THE COVENANT OF GRACE:

A THREAD THROUGH SCRIPTURE

A Commentary on the Confession of Faith
of the
Cumberland Presbyterian Church
Adopted in1984

HUBERT W. MORROW

Funded, in part, by your contributions to Our United Outreach.

This book was originally published in 1996.

Second printing June 2014.

ISBN-13: 978-0692244579
ISBN-10: 0692244573

CONTENTS

PREFACE

My serious study of the theological tradition of the Cumberland Presbyterian Church began in 1942, immediately after I became a candidate for the ministry in White River Presbytery, Arkansas Synod. The Committee on Literature and Theology of the presbytery assigned me to read *Theology Condensed,* by T.C. Blake, a prominent minister of the Cumberland Presbyterian Church in the 19th century. The book's title page says that it was "designed for advanced classes as a sabbath-school textbook, and for private instruction." I confess that at the time I found Blake rather heavy reading.

It may be, however, that it was this introduction to Cumberland Presbyterian theology which led me years later to write a doctoral dissertation at Vanderbilt University titled *The Background and Development of Cumberland Presbyterian Theology.* During the research for this project I became impressed with the theological audacity and creativity of 19th century Cumberland Presbyterians. That audacity and creativity have continued in the 1984 Confession of Faith.

My interest in doing a commentary on the new Confession of Faith comes out of this background of inquiry into the theological tradition of a people called Cumberland Presbyterians. The privilege of having been a member of the committee that wrote the 1984 Confession of Faith has given added incentive to this project. This book is dedicated to my wife, Virginia Sue Williamson Morrow (1920-1989). She was a gifted teacher and musician and a devout Christian who blessed the lives of a generation of young people and others in the Cumberland Presbyterian Church. Her love for the Cumberland Presbyterian Church and its traditions was reflected in the leadership which she exercised on all levels of church life, as a teacher, an elder, and a musician.

After recounting the stories of women and men of the covenant community who lived and died in the faith but are living still, the writer of Hebrews said, "Yet all of these, though they were commended for their faith, did not receive what was promised, since God had provided something better so that they would not, apart from us, be made perfect" (11:39-40). That faith in which Virginia Sue Williamson Morrow lived and died, yet is living still, and in which the people of God continue to live and die and live again, is God's gift of love in the covenant of grace.

Hubert W. Morrow

INTRODUCTION

Throughout its history the covenant community has confessed its faith in God, who called it into being. One of the community's early confessions appears in Deuteronomy 6:4-5: "Hear O Israel: The Lord is our God, the Lord alone. You shall love the Lord your God with all your heart, and with all your soul, and with all your might." When one of the scribes asked Jesus a question about the greatest commandment, Jesus responded by quoting from Deuteronomy 6:5, to which he added a quotation from Leviticus 19:18b: "You shall love your neighbor as yourself" (Mk. 12:31). Because of the impact of God's revelation in Jesus the Messiah on the covenant community, its confessions began to include references to the Christ event. More than half of the ancient confession called The Apostles' Creed is devoted to the Christ event.

Following the Protestant reformation in the 16th century, new confessions of faith emerged, reflecting the renewal of the church. At the heart of this renewal of the church was the recovery of the role of Scripture in its worship and life. The confessions that appeared in the Reformed/Presbyterian churches went beyond the brief summary of beliefs suitable for use in the liturgy of worship. They offered detailed outlines of the basic doctrines taught in Scripture and became guides for the study of Scripture. During the 16th and 17th centuries Presbyterian and Reformed churches in Europe and in the British Isles developed some fifteen confessions, catechisms, and other creedal statements.

The Westminster Confession and Catechism, published in England in 1647, have been most influential in Presbyterian churches in the United States. In a meeting of the Synod of Philadelphia in 1729, the colonial Presbyterian Church officially adopted the Westminster Confession as its creedal statement. The Scotch-Irish segment of the church wanted to make unconditional subscription to this document a test of orthodoxy. The New England segment of the church, led by the Reverend Jonathan Dickinson, opposed this rigid view, arguing that no document of human composure should usurp the position that belonged only to Scripture.

The Cumberland Presbyterian Church came out of that segment of the Presbyterian Church which held a less rigid view of the Westminster Confession. In the action taken on February 4, 1810 to reorganize Cumberland Presbytery, the presbytery adopted the Westminster Confession, "except the idea of fatality, that seems to be taught under the mysterious doctrine of predestination." The reasoning of McAdow, Ewing and King was that this doctrine did not have a solid basis in Scripture. At the same time, however, they agreed that persons who "can clearly receive the confession, without exception, shall not be required to make any."

Four years later, when Cumberland Presbytery had grown into three presbyteries and Cumberland Synod came into existence, the synod adopted a revised edition of the Westminster Confession. The revisions dealt primarily with the section on Divine Decrees, which contained the doctrines of predestination and limited atonement. This 1814 Confession of Faith represented a bold, creative development in the history of confessions in American Presbyterianism.

The 1814 revision of the Westminster Confession affirmed that the Reformed tradition should be understood as a tradition continually being reformed. It also affirmed the principle that in the formulation of the confessions of the church, the guiding principle should be their consistency with Scripture. Accordingly, the Preface to the 1814 revision of the Westminster Confession says of the revision, "If it speak not according to the Bible, let it be rejected."

The 1814 Confession of Faith served the church for almost seventy years. In the meantime a consensus was beginning to develop that this limited revision of the Westminster Confession did not adequately represent the teachings of the Bible as understood by Cumberland Presbyterians. This growing consensus led, in 1883, to the adoption of a major revision of the 1814 Confession of Faith. The Preface to the 1883 Confession of Faith concludes: "This book is now sent forth with strongest conviction that it is in accord with the word of God. Let it be tested, not by tradition, but by the Holy Scriptures, the only infallible rule of faith and practice."

The reaction of the Rev. J.M. Howard to the 1883 Confession of Faith reflected the distinctive Cumberland Presbyterian view of creedal statements. "Let it be understood, in short, that ours is not a fixed and changeless, but a progressive creed; and that through the decades we are to seek a more and more nearly exact statement of the truth revealed in Scripture, and believed by our own people."

A century later, in 1984, in faithfulness to this reforming principle, the Cumberland Presbyterian Church again revised its Confession of Faith. Again, but in an even more radical sense, Scripture guided the revision. The Introduction to the new Confession states: "The organizing principle of this confession of faith is to tell the story the Bible tells in the way the Bible tells it." The purpose of the new confession is said to be two-fold: "To provide a means whereby those who have been saved, redeemed, and reconciled by God through Jesus Christ in the power of the Holy Spirit understand and affirm their faith; and to bear witness to God's saving activity in such a way that those who have not been saved, redeemed, and reconciled might believe in Jesus Christ as Lord and Savior and experience salvation."

Though not expressly stated in the prefaces of the 1814 and the 1883 confessions, this two-fold purpose of a confession has always guided the use of the Cumberland Presbyterian Confession of Faith. It is not designed as a tool for the negative role of identifying heresy. Rather, it is designed as a tool for the positive role of nurturing the understanding of faith, and of equipping people of faith to become effective witnesses to the Gospel.

Cumberland Presbyterian confessions of faith have been relatively brief, concise statements of basic beliefs about God, derived from Scripture. In reflecting on the fuller meaning of these concise statements, many people have found it helpful to have a companion book that is of the nature of a commentary on the confession. Richard Beard, Professor of Systematic Theology, Cumberland University, authored such a commentary on the 1814 Confession of Faith, entitled *Why I Am a Cumberland Presbyterian*. In a similar fashion, E.K. Reagin, President of Bethel College and professor in its theological department, wrote a commentary on the 1883 Confession of Faith. Entitled *What Cumberland Presbyterians Believe,* it remains today the most widely known and read book on the Cumberland Presbyterian theological tradition.

The Covenant of Grace is a sequel to these earlier books. It takes its title from the dominant theological theme of the 1984 Confession of Faith, and emphasizes what may be its most important difference from the two previous confessions. The 1814 Confession of Faith followed the Westminster Confession in claiming that God's original covenant with the human family was a covenant of law, or works. According to that confession, when Adam and Eve failed the covenant of law, God established a second covenant, the covenant of grace. The 1883 Confession of Faith retained this two covenant schema, but redefined the covenant of law in significant ways and muted its effects throughout the confession.

The 1984 Confession of Faith drops all references to the covenant of law or works, on the grounds that there is no solid evidence in Scripture for such a covenant. Rather, it affirms that the first and only covenant which God has had with the human family is the covenant of grace. This is the reason that the Introduction to this confession says that John 3:16 is the essence of the biblical story, and it is the reason that this text stands as the opening statement of the confession. John 3:16 is the essence of the covenant of grace.

An extensive list of Scripture texts keyed to each section demonstrates the biblical grounding of the 1984 Confession of Faith. Persons undertaking a study of the Confession of Faith should read these Scriptures as part of the study of each section. These lists are far more extensive than those contained in the two previous confessions. The biblical selections do not serve as proof texts for the doctrinal statements. Rather, they are a beginning point for a more extensive study of Scripture, using the Confession of Faith as a guide.

In a very real sense, this commentary on the 1984 Confession of Faith is an interpretation of these and other texts within the overall framework of the covenant of grace. In this commentary the writer hopes to make it clear what it means to read and understand Scripture solely in terms of the covenant of grace.

(Note: All Scripture quoted in this book is from the New Revised Standard Version, unless otherwise indicated.)

CHAPTER 1

GOD SPEAKS AND ACTS

Read Confession of Faith 1.01-1.03; 1.13-1.22 and Scriptures listed for these sections.

Introduction

When Christians confess that they believe in God, they do so out of experiences in which they have encountered God as one who speaks and acts. Scripture does not suggest that persons find God as a consequence of their searches. On the contrary, Scripture shows that more often than not, persons try to run away and escape from God. This is because all persons are sinners, like Adam and Eve, and do not want to confront the holy God.

When the Confession of Faith says that God speaks and acts, it affirms that persons know God through revelation in experiences of encounter, which God initiates. On page after page in Scripture, God says and does something. It is through the word and act of God that persons come to understand something about the nature and will of God.

This is not to deny a certain mystical knowledge of God, which may come through reflection and meditation; but the possibility of this kind of knowledge usually follows experiences in which God confronts the person in word and deed. Unless the knowledge of God is rooted in God's revelation in word and deed, it tends to be speculative and abstract. This kind of knowledge may be appropriate for philosophical discussions, but for the most part it is incidental to faith and discipleship. The claim that persons know God through God's word and act is analogous to the way persons come to know each other. One may learn certain things (size, hair color, sex) about another person by observation. A third person may communicate some facts—date and place of birth, names of father and mother, place of employment. Despite all these facts that may be acquired in these ways, two people really get to know each other in encounter—when they interact with each other in word and deed. This is because in such a relationship they begin to reveal themselves to each other through word and deed. The most important knowledge of persons comes through free and open self revelation. Such knowledge is not available to the other on demand, for by its very nature it cannot be coerced. Though this analogy may be helpful in understanding how persons know God, like all analogies and language from human experience, it has limitations and should not be pushed to the extreme when applied to God. However, it is an analogy that is drawn from both Old and New Testament Scripture. An examination of certain accounts of divine-human encounters in Scripture will confirm the importance of this analogy.

The Divine-Human Encounter

The story of Adam and Eve in Genesis 3:8-10 suggests that there was a daily encounter between God and the persons created in the divine image. Adam and Eve heard "the sound of the Lord God walking in the garden at the time of the evening breeze." Reference to the "sound of the Lord God walking" is clearly figurative language, but it suggests action. Once they became aware of God's presence, the man and woman heard God speak, "Where are you?" This scene is played out many times in the divine-human drama, to which Scripture gives witness. God comes looking for persons, those creatures made in the divine image. Often God finds persons hiding, because they know themselves to be sinners, those who have rebelled against God. When they become aware of God's presence and hear God speak, they may try to avoid a face to face encounter.

Exodus 3:1-6 provides another biblical example. While a man named Moses was keeping the flock of his father-in-law, he saw a most unusual sight, a "bush was blazing, yet it was not consumed." This sign caught Moses' attention, and when "he had turned aside to see, God called to him out of the bush." This episode recalls a phrase in the hymn which reflects a sensitivity to God's presence in the natural world: "In the rustling grass I hear him pass, he speaks to me everywhere." Later, when Moses and the Israelites had escaped from Egypt, they discovered that Pharaoh and his army were in hot pursuit. Caught between the Egyptian army on one side and the Red Sea on the other side, the Israelites were ready to give up. Moses urged the people to "stand firm, and see the deliverance that the Lord (would) accomplish" (Ex. 14:13). It was in this experience of deliverance that all of Israel encountered God. In the Passover Feast, Israel remembered the exodus, and celebrated a God who acts.

After the appearance of the prophetic movement in the biblical story, God begins to speak through prophets. The prophetic period ushered in the use of a phrase that became important in all subsequent biblical history. The phrase was "the word of God." Amos, the first prophet whose message survives in written form, said to Israel, "Hear this word that the Lord has spoken" (Am. 3:1). Spoken through the prophet, the word of

God is a power that could both destroy and heal. Isaiah 55:11 affirms that the word of God will accomplish God's purpose and succeed in the thing for which it is sent into the world.

In the New Testament, the word of God spoken through the prophets becomes the Word of God made flesh in Jesus the Messiah. Word and action become one in this ultimate revelation of God to the human family. As the writer of Hebrews puts it, "Long ago God spoke to our ancestors in many and various ways by the prophets, but in these last days he has spoken to us by a Son" (1:1-2). The word of God spoken in the life, death and resurrection of Jesus the Messiah is called by the book of Revelation both the first and the last word of God, the Alpha and the Omega, the word of creation and the word of redemption.

Thus it is that the Confession of Faith says, "The one living God who is Father, Son and Holy Spirit, the Holy Trinity speaks through . . . the events of nature and history, apostles, prophets, . . . but uniquely in Jesus Christ, the word made flesh" (1.02). This means that the doctrine of the Trinity is not something arrived at through speculation about the nature of God. It is an affirmation of faith concerning the kind of God whom the people of the covenant community have encountered and continue to encounter in the word and act of God.

Encounter in Nature

The psalmist said that persons may encounter God and hear God speak through the natural world. "The heavens are telling the glory of God; and the firmament proclaims his handiwork" (19:1). Speaking of the whole human family, Paul wrote, "For what can be known about God is plain to them, because God has shown it to them. Ever since the creation of the world his eternal power and divine nature, invisible though they are, have been understood and seen through the things he has made" (Rom. 1:19-20).

The process of reasoning is a commonly understood manner in which God's revelation appears to persons. This process has found form in what some call the arguments or proofs for the existence of God. As an example, many say that when one examines the intricate design and order everywhere evident in the natural world, one must conclude that some higher power was the source of this creation. Scripture knows nothing of this kind of formal reasoning as the process through which God is revealed in nature. The approach in Scripture is more direct. The Israelites were able to cross the Red Sea on dry land, because "the Lord drove the sea back by a strong east wind all night, and formed the sea into dry land" (Ex. 14:21). Speaking of God's creativity in the natural world, the psalmist wrote, "You make springs gush forth in the valleys; . . . giving drink to every wild animal. . . . You cause the grass to grow for the cattle, and plants for people to use" (104:10, 14). These affirmations suggest that God does not wait to be discovered at the end of a process of reasoning about the natural world, but actively reveals the divine nature in the structure and events of nature.

Scripture knows nothing about a closed natural order, into which God may enter only when this order is suspended. God, who dwells in eternity is able to enter continually and freely into the realm of time and space. Accordingly, the Confession affirms, "The whole creation remains open to God's direct activity" (1.14). The concept of a miracle as something God does directly in the world, suspending the natural order, is foreign to Scripture. This definition is relatively modern and was developed by theologians after the advent of modern science. They were concerned that the concept of the world as a self-contained system of causes and effects, which the physics of Isaac Newton described, left no room for the activity of God.

The biblical view affirms that what Newton described is exactly what God is doing in the natural world every day and night. In the words of the psalmist, night comes because God sets up a tent in the heavens and puts the sun under it. When God causes the sun to rise, it comes out of the tent "like a bridegroom from his wedding canopy" (19:4, 5). Because God is everywhere and always doing things in the natural world, every natural event both usual and unusual may become a sign or wonder. Events of the natural world become signs when they point persons to God. They are called wonders when people stop and wonder at them, asking questions about what these things mean in relation to divine purposes. There is yet another aspect, one pertaining to the nature of human beings, of God's revelation in nature. In Romans, Paul says that Gentiles "show that what the law requires is written on their hearts, to which their own conscience also bears witness"(2:15). The Confession of Faith identifies this as the moral law which is "woven into the fabric of the universe and is binding upon all persons" (1.19). This built-in moral sensitivity or capacity for moral decisions is a medium for God's revelation (1.20). It is the ultimate source of all civil law.

God's revelation in nature is active. It is what God is doing and saying. God the creator is still creating, doing and saying new things. Scripture knows nothing of a static world, something finished and running on its own, like a clock, that simply exists to be observed by persons. God's revelation in nature comes when persons encounter the living God everywhere doing and saying things through natural events.

As the Psalmist noted, things in nature don't actually talk, "Yet their voice goes out through all the earth, and their words to the end of the world" (19:3, 4).

This is, in part, what the Confession means when it says, "God's providence is sufficiently displayed to be known and experienced, but at the same time, it partakes of divine mystery and is the occasion for wonder, praise and thanksgiving" (1.18). This is so even though it includes what persons have called natural evils.

Encounter in History

The Confession of Faith affirms that "God . . . speaks through . . . the events of nature and *history*" (1.02, italics added). Both nature and history are arenas in which God is doing things and saying things. The term history refers to those events that are caused directly or indirectly by the decisions and actions of persons. Though for purposes of analysis the two realms of nature and history are separated, they are nevertheless interconnected. God's speaking and acting often occur simultaneously in both realms because all history occurs in the world, in the realm of time and space.

That God is speaking and acting in all events of history, both good and bad, is one of the most important claims in Scripture. The providence of God includes both the realms of nature and history, but it is in the realm of history that difficulties of understanding are most common. It is in history that God works in and through the actions of persons. (See COF 1.14.) The Confession affirms that this includes "all who trust God" and "all who do not trust God" (1.16).

Scripture sometimes describes historical events as done by persons, and sometimes as done by God. At the same time, in those events ascribed to persons, whether good or bad, Scripture affirms that God is working, doing and saying things. Similarly, those events which are ascribed to God are also things which persons do in the exercise of their God-given freedom. Scripture does not identify any historical events in which God is working which do not in one way or another involve the free decisions of persons.

An element of mystery exists in the revelation of God in and through the events of nature. Reflection on God's revelation in and through the events of history heightens this mystery. Christian theology has demonstrated counter tendencies toward an elimination of this mystery. One tendency has been to define the sovereignty of God in such a way as to arrive at the conclusion that God determines all events of history that come to pass. Such thinking eliminates meaningful human freedom and reduces historical events to a kind of puppet show, with God pulling the strings. The other tendency has been to define human freedom in such a way as to reduce God to an observer of what persons do, becoming active only after the fact, rewarding persons who do what is good and punishing those who do what is evil. There may be a further affirmation that God functions in a kind of clean-up role, bringing something good out of the mess persons have made.

An alternative to both of these views affirms that in the same historical event persons are making free decisions and God is working to accomplish the divine purpose. It is immediately clear that in this view the mystery of how God works in the events of history is far greater than of how God works in the events of nature. Careful reflection on the record of historical events in Scripture will confirm that this is exactly what is happening. People are freely saying and doing things, and God is saying and doing things in these events of history.

An analogy from the dynamics of human relationships may be helpful in understanding how both persons and God are acting in the same event. A good parent does not simply leave a child alone to make his or her own decisions, entering the picture only to mete out rewards or punishments. The parent acts to communicate to the child a sense of right and wrong, and continually gives the child love and support. The parent may, even without the knowledge of the child, alter some of the external circumstances in which the decisions of the child will occur. At the same time, a sensitive parent both leaves the child free to make decisions and remains active in what the child does. Even when a rebellious child demands absolute freedom and tries to go it alone, the moral character and compassionate love of the parent continue as a strong presence in whatever the child does. Jesus used a parable to illustrate his understanding of these issues. He said that if earthly parents know how to deal with their children in a wise and compassionate manner, respecting their freedom and individuality, God knows even better how to deal with all those creatures made in the divine image. (See Lu. 11:13).

The exodus event has already been cited as an example of encounter between God and persons. It is an example, also, of how the same event is both what people do in their freedom, and what God does in and through free human actions. The leading human characters in the exodus event were Pharaoh and Moses. They made decisions and took actions, yet God was working in and through what both of them decided and did.

The destruction of the national state of Israel, first by the Assyrians then by the Babylonians, was clearly the work of ambitious kings who were bent on establishing their empires. Nevertheless, the prophets saw that in the free decisions and actions of these kings God was disciplining Israel and calling the nation back to the mission described in Exodus 19:5-6. According to Isaiah, the king of Assyria was "the rod of (God's) anger"; yet this was not what the king understood he was doing."It [was] in his mind to destroy, and to cut off nations not a few," and thereby extend the boundaries of his empire. (See Isa. 10:5-7; see also Jer. 7:1-34 for an interpretation of the Babylonian invasion.)

In addition, the latter chapters of Isaiah claim that in the destruction of the national state of Israel God acted to disperse Israel among the nations to become a light to the Gentiles. The events of the Day of Pentecost, recorded in Acts 2, and the subsequent spread of the Gospel throughout the Roman empire confirm this claim. Even in the death of Stephen, and the persecutions of the followers of Jesus which resulted, God acted to accomplish the divine purpose.

Finally, the one series of events which illuminate all events in which God says and does things is the birth, life, death and resurrection of Jesus the Messiah. This is one of the reasons that it is important to affirm the true humanity of Jesus. In his humanity, Jesus said and did things freely. At the same time, in and through what this man freely did and said, God was incarnate, speaking the word of judgment and bringing the gift of redemption.

Encounter in a Covenant of Grace

Classical theological statements about God, particularly from the Greek period of early church history, contained lists of attributes that might be described as abstract superlatives. God was said to be omnipotent (all powerful), omniscient (all wise), immutable (unchanging), eternal (without beginning or end), self-existent, and infinite in justice, holiness, goodness and truth.

Although the Confession affirms such attributes, it is significant that the list is prefaced by the statement that God "is holy love" (1.01). The very first section of the Confession affirms what its preface states: that John 3:16 contains the heart of the biblical story. In a very direct and forthright manner, I John 4:8 gives testimony to this central claim: "Whoever does not love does not know God, for God is love." This radical claim means that God's power is the power of love, God's wisdom is the wisdom of love, God's justice is the justice of love, God's goodness is the goodness of love, God's truth is the truth of love. The confession that God is holy love has important corollaries for the nature of divine-human relations.It suggests that God is personal in nature, that God is a covenant-making God. God, who is holy love, establishes a covenant of grace with the whole creation, particularly with those creatures made in the divine image. The Confession says, "By word and action God invites persons into a covenant relationship and that "God promises to be faithful to the covenant, and to make all who believe his people" (1.03). This statement announces God's covenant of grace as a central theme of Scripture. It is a covenant manifested in God's works of creation, judgment and redemption. The creation story does not make explicit reference to God's covenant, but implies it in the divine affirmation of the essential goodness of all things and God's satisfaction with the creation (Gen. 1:31). The covenant of grace in creation is present in God's promise to sustain and continually renew the creation. Psalm 104 speaks of God's loving relationship to the whole creation. Even "the young lions roar for their prey, seeking their food from God" (v. 21). The psalmist goes on to affirm both the absolute dependence on God of all created things and God's covenant promise to continually sustain and renew all living things. "When you hide your face, they are dismayed; when you take away their breath, they die and return to dust. When you send forth your spirit they are created; and you renew the face of the ground" (vv. 29-30).

In a marvelous poem in Isaiah describing the wonder and magnitude of God's creation, the writer concludes with an affirmation about how God sustains and cares for the creation. Of the stars the poet says that God "brings out their host and numbers them, calling them all by name, because he is great in strength, mighty in power, *not one is missing*" (Isa. 40:26, italics added).

The covenant of grace which God has with the world is implicit in the nature of God's relationship with Adam and Eve. God created them for fellowship with God in a relationship of love and trust. This is the essential meaning of the claim that they were made in the image of God. God's faithfulness to the covenant as it pertained to Adam and Eve becomes evident not only in provisions to sustain them by putting them in a garden with a tree of life, but in daily fellowship with them "in the garden at the time of the evening breeze" (Gen. 3:8).

Neither the rebellion of these creatures made for fellowship with God, nor the impact of their rebellion on the whole creation destroyed God's covenant bond. God affirmed the covenant with Noah following the near destruction of all living things because of evil. (See Gen. 9:8-17.) This is the first explicit use in the biblical story of the term covenant. The idea of a covenant reveals the nature of God's absolutely unconditional promise to act on behalf of the whole creation. At God's initiative, and in God's absolutely unconditioned freedom, God affirmed the covenant and promised to sustain every living creature on the earth. The sign of the covenant was the rainbow, a sign of God's faithfulness and of hope for the whole creation.

Because of the sin of the creatures made in God's image, and because of the impact of their sin on the rest of the creation, God expressed faithfulness to the covenant not simply in a promise to sustain and renew but also to redeem the creation. The problem of sin began with the rebellion of persons against God, so the promise of redemption began first with the human family. The Confession affirms that, in faithfulness to the covenant, God created a covenant community, composed of those who respond to God's love in repentance and faith. God determined to work in and through this community of redeemed people to give testimony to God's covenant love for all people. (See COF 1.03; Gen. 12:1-3; 17:3 5.)

Encounter with God: Father, Son, Holy Spirit

In the context of God's covenant relationship with the whole creation, and, in particular, with creatures made in the image of God, affirmations about the attributes of God spring forth. This covenant relationship is the context of all that God says and does in the world. It is in this context that the living God seeks to be known as Father, Son and Holy Spirit. The doctrine of the Trinity does not derive from a metaphysical analysis of the being of God. Rather, it is a testimony by the covenant community about the nature of God revealed in the speaking and acting of God within the covenant of grace.

An ancient confession of the covenant community begins, "Hear, O Israel: The Lord our God is one Lord" (Deut. 6:4, RSV). This became the confession of the faith community throughout the biblical story. After the birth, life, death and resurrection of Jesus of Nazareth, his followers believed that he was the Messiah of which the prophets spoke. Followers of Jesus added this claim to the ancient confession from Deuteronomy, and thus provided a clearer revelation of the doctrine of the Trinity. Using the concept of the word of God developed by the great prophets, the Gospel of John refers to Jesus the Messiah as the Word. At the same time, the Word was both with God, and was God. This Word, who was God, "became flesh and lived among us" as Jesus of Nazareth. (See Jn. 1:1-18.) In his second letter to the Corinthians, Paul gave a strong witness to the incarnation of God in Jesus the Messiah: "God was *in* Christ reconciling the world to himself" (2 Cor. 5:19, italics added). These affirmations in the Gospel of John and in the Pauline letters clearly grew out of some of the things Jesus taught his disciples toward the end of his ministry, but more particularly out of what the Holy Spirit later revealed to them concerning the meaning of the whole Christ event. However, the most frequent term used in the New Testament to describe the relation of Jesus the Messiah to God is that of Son. Even the Gospel of John, which has the most direct witness to the incarnation of God in Jesus of Nazareth, says that "God so loved the world, that he gave his only Son" (3:16). The nature of the relationship which the terms Father and Son suggest led some in the early church to conclude that the Son was a subordinate being, under God the Father. The Council of Nicea condemned this view as a heresy in 325 A.D., but it persisted for centuries in the church. It is understandable, even today, how the ordinary meaning of the terms father and son may consciously or unconsciously imply a subordinate relationship of Jesus Christ the Son to God the Father. One way of counteracting the influence of this implied subordinate relationship is to consciously use the terms God the Father and God the Son. In Hebrew culture, unless a family included a son who could continue the family name, the family was said to be cut off from the land of the living. In a sense not present in our culture, a son was the embodiment of his father. In theological terms, God the Son was the embodiment (incarnation) of God the Father.

The doctrine of the Trinity finds completion with affirmations about God the Holy Spirit. The Old Testament includes many references to the Spirit of God, beginning with the creation story which states that "the Spirit of God was moving over the face of the waters" (Gen. 1:2, RSV). In many, if not most of its instances in the Old Testament, the term Spirit is a synonym for God.

The New Testament begins to refer to the Spirit of God as the Holy Spirit, a term Isaiah and the Psalmist also used. From the stories of the conception of Jesus in the womb of Mary by the Holy Spirit to the final chapter of Revelation, God the Holy Spirit is the powerful presence of God in the life of the covenant community.

Throughout his ministry, Jesus claimed to be acting in the power of the Holy Spirit. His awareness of the Holy Spirit became clearly evident at his baptism, when the Scripture says that the Holy Spirit descended on him. According to the Gospel of John, Jesus gave the Holy Spirit to the apostles. It was the event of Pentecost, however, which marked the beginning of a new and unique presence of the Holy Spirit in the life of the covenant community.

The entire book of Acts associates the gift of the Holy Spirit to believers with their baptism. Beginning with the metaphor Jesus used in his conversation with Nicodemus, new converts experienced being born of the Spirit. This understanding of the work of the Holy Spirit is compatible with the use of the term in the Old Testament, which understood Spirit (wind or breath) to be the principle of life. The ritual of baptism at Pentecost, which seems to have been in the name of Christ, soon became baptism "in the name of the Father, Son, and Holy Spirit." (See Acts 2:38; Mt. 28:19.)

The concept of God the Holy Spirit and the biblical use of the metaphor of being born of the Holy Spirit opens up a profound dimension of understanding the Trinity. The Bible explicitly refers to God as heavenly Father. Though the actual term is not used, the claim that God is also heavenly Mother is unmistakable in the metaphor of birth in and by the Holy Spirit. Fathers share in conceiving children, but mothers give them birth. Both the Scripture and the history of the church confirm this understanding of God the Holy Spirit by the use of the dove, a feminine image, as a metaphor for the Holy Spirit. (See Mt. 3:16; Mk. 1:10; Lu. 3:22; Jn. 1:32.)

The doctrine of the Trinity is difficult to understand. The early councils of the church struggled to find language that would affirm the oneness of God, while recognizing the distinctions implied in God the Father, God the Son and God the Holy Spirit. Various metaphors enable the human mind to grasp something of this dimension of the mystery of God's speaking and acting in the world. Some people, weary of the effort to understand, may say, "We are not supposed to understand." Perhaps a better way of describing an appropriate response of sinful, finite creatures standing in the presence of the mystery of the holy Trinity, is to "take off our shoes" and to acknowledge that we are in the presence of God. The doctrine of the Trinity is nowhere explained in Scripture, yet has clearly defined roots in Scripture. Potential pitfalls exist in any understanding of the doctrine of the Trinity. First, language must never compromise the essential oneness of God. Second, the distinctions within God as revealed in God's word and work, represented by the terms Father, Son and Holy Spirit, do not imply three autonomous persons. Third, in any understanding of the Father, Son, and Holy Spirit, the work of one should not be set against the work of the others or regarded as unique or peculiar to one and not the others. Any one or all three terms make reference to God. An encouragement to this way of thinking may be to say, not simply "Father, Son, or Holy Spirit," but "God the Father, God the Son, and God the Holy Spirit."

What Cumberland Presbyterians confess about the revelation of God in word and act derives from what God reveals in Scripture. Scripture performs a vital role as the authoritative medium for God's revelation.

For Discussion

1. What are some of the events of nature and/or history in which you have encountered God? Describe some of your encounters and what you learned from them.
2. What do we mean when we say that God "speaks to us"? We sing hymns with words such as "Speak, Lord, in the Stillness" and "Lord, Speak to Me, That I May Speak." What are we saying about our expectations of God's presence in our midst? Do we really expect an audible response? If not, then what?
3. How have you "seen God" doing things?
4. Assuming that, in any given historical event, both God and persons are saying and doing things, reflect on the role of the divine and the human in each of the following circumstances or events:
    a. the Holocaust.
    b. floods, earthquakes or other natural events which disrupt human life.
    c. changing world situations, especially the changes in Eastern Europe and the move toward nuclear disarmament in that hemisphere, coupled with our increasing awareness of the presence of and potential for nuclear weapons in Asia and in the Middle East.
5. What does it mean to you personally that God is bound to the whole creation in a covenant of grace? Is this a comforting or an unsettling concept? How would human life differ from what we know if we thought of humanity as bound to God's covenant in the same way we think of God's being bound to it?
6. What is the significance of the doctrine of the Trinity for your personal faith and understanding? What images and pictures help the doctrine of the Trinity become more meaningful for you? What are your responses to phrases such as "Creator, Redeemer, and Sustainer" in addition to "Father, Son, and Spirit"?
7. After reading this chapter, are you thankful for our God who acts? Or might you prefer a God who is through acting and retires to a comfortable distance from the creation?

CHAPTER 2

TESTIMONY TO GOD'S WORD AND ACT

Read Confession of Faith 1.04-1.09 and Scriptures listed for these sections.

Introduction

The Confession of Faith claims that God speaks through "the events of nature and history, apostles, prophets, evangelists, pastors, teachers, but uniquely in Jesus Christ, the Word made flesh" (1.02). God's revelation takes on the nature of personal encounter. Scripture serves as a means of demonstrating the claim that God speaks and acts. We turn now to the nature and authority of Scripture as the account of God's speaking and acting, and to a description of how the church approaches the study of the Scripture.

The Confession of Faith says, "God's words and actions are witnessed to by the covenant community in the scriptures of the Old and New Testaments" (1.04). The community of faith interprets and uses Scripture in its life and remembers that the Bible contains the witness of faith by people of the covenant community throughout the ages.

A Testimony of the Covenant Community

Scripture is a witness by the covenant community to what God is saying and doing in the events of nature and history. It is a testimony by members of the covenant community who encountered God, and responded to God in repentance and faith. Scripture is essentially a historical document. The Introduction to the Confession refers to "the story the Bible tells" (p. xv). The story is about people, primarily of the covenant community, and about their experiences in the events of nature and history. Imbedded in the biblical record of these events is a testimony of faith about what God was saying and doing in and through the events. For the most part, the historical accuracy of the accounts may find corroboration in extra-biblical sources. However, the claim as to what these events mean, what God was saying and doing in the events, is the witness of faith by the covenant community.

Two examples, the Old Testament account of the exodus and the New Testament record of the Christ event, will illustrate both the historical nature of Scripture, and its nature as a testimony of faith. The exodus is the central event of the Old Testament, and the Christ event is central not only to the New Testament but to the entire Bible.

Let us suppose that a reporter for the *Cairo Daily* had been present to write stories about the exodus. As a good reporter, he would have dealt with the facts. The following might have been the essence of a series of stories that he prepared:

> A man named Moses showed up one day and demanded that Pharaoh free the Hebrew slaves. This Moses was a Hebrew who had been reared as the adopted son of an Egyptian princess. He had left Egypt several years earlier under suspicion of murder. Pharaoh dismissed the request of Moses as both impertinent and ludicrous. Moses threatened Pharaoh, saying that his refusal would have dire consequences for the country.
>
> By coincidence, a series of unusual events have occurred. Egyptian authorities have given their own explanation of these events, but Moses has claimed that a god named Yahweh caused them to occur. Pharaoh was not convinced by the explanation of Moses, but finally agreed that the Hebrew slaves would be permitted to leave. Actually, it appears that this was a maneuver to expose their leaders, so that the rebellion could be put down. They would be permitted to leave, but the army would follow, to capture and return them to Egypt.
>
> The plan was working beautifully. The Hebrews left, going east toward the Red Sea. Pharaoh and his army soon followed, and had the slaves cornered at the Red Sea, with all escape routes cut off. A strong east wind began to blow across the Red Sea, literally drying it up in the section immediately before the Hebrew slaves. They scurried across with the Egyptian army in hot pursuit. The chariots of Pharaoh's army became mired in the wet sands of the sea bed, and, before they could escape, the wind stopped and the waters of the sea returned. The entire army was drowned, but the slaves escaped into the desert.

Thus ends the story by the reporter for the *Cairo Daily*. In recounting these same events in writings that eventually became part of the Torah (Law), the people of the covenant community reported the same facts, but wove into their story a witness concerning what God was doing and saying. Obviously, the people had not seen God anywhere doing anything or heard God saying anything. In fact, all that people saw and heard was either an event of nature or an event of history.

From the point of view of an objective observer, these events were just that. The events of nature, though unusual, nevertheless involved things in nature—hail, gnats, flies, locusts, an east wind. The events of history were what people were doing—governments oppressing minorities, minorities crying out in their oppression, radical individuals causing trouble by encouraging minorities to think about being free from oppression, leaders in government playing for time.

It was the eye of faith which saw God working in these events. It was the ear of faith that heard God saying, "I have observed the misery of my people who are in Egypt . . . . I have come down to deliver them from the Egyptians" (Ex. 3: 7, 8). It was out of such seeing and hearing, the Confession of Faith affirms, that persons of the covenant community gave testimony to the mighty acts of God (1.04). The account of the events, interwoven with the testimony of faith, became what is called Scripture.

Change the scene from Egypt to Palestine, and to a time centuries later. The reporter works for the *Jerusalem Times*. The following is the essence of the story the reporter wrote on special assignment:

> A man named Jesus, from Nazareth, appeared at the river Jordan where a prophet named John was preaching and baptizing. Jesus went forward and was baptized, and soon afterward became an itinerant rabbi, teaching in synagogues or wherever people would gather to listen. The religious leaders, particularly in Jerusalem, didn't like what Jesus was teaching, because he criticized their religion of law. Instead, he offered what came to be called a religion of grace.
>
> Jesus taught that God dealt with people like a loving Father, rather than a stern judge. The following incident illustrates what he taught about the difference in a religion of law and a religion of grace: One day Jesus encountered a group of people about to stone a woman accused of adultery, as the Law provided. Jesus challenged anyone who was without sin to cast the first stone. As the crowd faded away, Jesus forgave the woman and encouraged her to change her lifestyle. The religious authorities in Jerusalem regarded the religion of grace which Jesus taught and practiced as a dangerous heresy and began to search for ways to suppress or eliminate him. When they learned that some of his followers believed him to be the Messiah, the religious authorities decided to report him to the Roman governor as a dangerous revolutionary.
>
> Jesus was arrested and taken before Pilate, the Roman governor. Though Pilate found no credible evidence that Jesus was

plotting to overthrow Roman rule in Palestine, he gave in to the demands of the religious authorities and had Jesus executed on a cross outside Jerusalem. Three days after the execution and burial of Jesus, his tomb was found empty. Some of his followers were suspected of stealing the body and claiming that Jesus had risen from the grave.

This ends the story by the reporter for the *Jerusalem Times*. Later, written accounts of essentially this same story circulated among the followers of Jesus. These writers wove many of the teachings of Jesus and some affirmations of faith about who Jesus was into their story. These followers said that he was the Messiah, of whom the prophets had spoken. They claimed that his gracious deeds were a sign that the Kingdom of God, the rule of God on earth, was a present reality. Moreover, they asserted that Jesus the Messiah had established and was ruling over the Kingdom of God on earth. Unlike the kings of this world, however, he ruled not by power and might, but by teaching and serving. Most astounding of all, his followers claimed that his death on the cross was not a defeat as first thought, but a manifestation of God's self-giving, suffering love for sinful people. One of his followers named Paul called the death of Jesus a manifestation of God's power in weakness (1 Cor. 1:27). The resurrection of Jesus from the dead was the climactic evidence that in him God had destroyed and was destroying the power of evil in the world. Through the resurrection of Jesus the Christ, God would liberate the world from bondage to sin and death. As in the case of the exodus of Israel from Egypt, all of these affirmations of faith came from people of the covenant community. They had the eyes and ears of faith to see and hear what God was doing and saying in the history of this man Jesus of Nazareth. This is what the Confession means when it says that "God's words and actions" are "witnessed to by the covenant community" (1.04).

This witness of faith by persons in the covenant community concerning God's words and acts is essentially what believers mean by the inspiration of the writers of the Scriptures. The Confession states, "God inspired persons of the covenant community to write the scriptures" (1.05). Indeed, Scriptures themselves support this claim. (See 2 Tim. 3:16).

Any reliable reporter could have recorded the facts of the story of the Bible. However, only persons whom God inspired could have said what these things meant and continue to mean. Understanding the inspiration of Scripture is fundamental to establishing the truth of the theological interpretations which the writers wove into the record of facts.

The Authority of Scripture

The Confession of Faith says that "the scriptures are an infallible rule of faith and practice, the authoritative guide for Christian living" (1.05). The key to understanding this claim lies in the statement which precedes it: "In and through the scriptures God speaks about creation, sin, judgment, salvation, the church and the growth of believers" (1.05). The authority of Scripture pertains to what it says about these topics. Efforts to make Scripture an authority on every subject may be well intentioned, but are misguided. In an attempt to bring the authority of Scripture into sharper focus, the Confession says that "the scriptures are the infallible rule of faith and practice," with respect to creation, sin, judgment, salvation, the church and the growth of believers (1.05, italics added). The term faith has meaning on at least two levels. The most common use of the term in Scripture is in reference to a human response to God's grace. The term is sometimes used in a secondary sense, however, as a reference to the body of beliefs which Christians hold concerning God. Use of the term practice refers to the lifestyle appropriate for the Christian. The best way to comprehend the theological meaning of faith is to examine the use of the term in the context of human relations. In its most fundamental sense in human relations, faith means to trust in, as to trust in a person. Carrying the meaning one step further, faith involves entrusting one's self to another person from whom one has been alienated. Faith becomes more than an expression of confidence in the dependability of a person. It is a response to the forgiveness and acceptance received from another person. It is being drawn to the other person by his or her acts of self-giving love. Ultimately, faith is a surrender of one's self to the other person.

A theological understanding of faith begins with a clear grasp of the human predicament of alienation from God. Paul describes this situation in Romans 5:10 by saying that persons are enemies of God. In Romans 5:12 and 6:6, Paul speaks of the predicament as a bondage to sin and death. Ephesians 2:1, 12 describes the human predicament both as being "dead through the trespasses and sin," and as being "strangers to the covenants of promise, having no hope and without God in the world." In this context, Ephesians 2:8 describes faith as a gift of God, a gift that enables a person to respond to God's grace. It is the experience of the grace of God, the forgiving and accepting love of God, by which the dead person is raised to new life through Jesus the Messiah.

Nowhere else, except in Scripture, can one find the authoritative, infallible rule of faith in this sense. Nowhere else can one find the true account of how the miracle of faith occurs. Nowhere else but in Scripture can one find the Good News that God in Christ forgives and accepts the sinner and sets the sinner free from bondage to the sin and death of self-centeredness. Nowhere else but in Scripture does one find both the good news of the grace of God, and the good news of the gift of faith by which one becomes able to respond to God's grace.

The term the Christian faith illustrates a secondary meaning of faith. Here faith refers to that body of beliefs about God which the covenant community derives from Scripture. To say that the Scripture is the infallible rule of faith in this sense is simply to acknowledge the essential nature of the biblical story. The Bible is the medium through which the covenant community gives witness to the words and actions of God. From a study of this witness, one may derive true beliefs about God.

The fact that the Bible is the one and only infallible source of beliefs about God does not insure that persons will always formulate these beliefs correctly. This is the reason, as noted in the Introduction to the Confession, that Cumberland Presbyterians have remained open to periodic revisions of the Confession of Faith. "All testimony to Jesus Christ must be tested by the Scriptures which are the only unfailing and authoritative word for Christian faith, growth, and practice" (COF, p. xv). This testing is an ongoing process.

The Confession also says that the Scriptures are "the only infallible rule of . . . practice, the authoritative guide for Christian living." The terms "practice" and "Christian living" are intended as synonyms, as are "infallible rule" and "authoritative guide." It is interesting that the quotation from the Introduction cited above inserts the word "growth" between faith and practice. The process of growth in grace and in the knowledge of God is fundamental to practice.

One approach to using the Scriptures as a rule for practice, or as a guide for Christian living is to extract from the Scriptures a set of rules by which to live. In the time of Jesus, this was the approach of the scribes and Pharisees. From the Law and the Prophets, they extracted a set of laws or rules for governing conduct. They went on to indicate that God would reward those who kept the rules and punish those who broke them.

A version of the legalism of the scribes and Pharisees has sometimes arisen in the Christian church. According to this legalistic or works-based religion, the lifestyle of the Christian finds definition in terms of a set of rules, things that Christians should and should not do. More often than not the emphasis is on prohibited behaviors. Apart from the difficulty of determining which rules found in Scripture are applicable to the Christian life, the appeal to the motives of reward and punishment seems inconsistent with the revelation of God in Jesus the Messiah. If anything is clear in the teaching of Jesus, it is that he rejected the legalistic religion of the scribes and Pharisees.

A different approach is to view the Scripture as the infallible or authoritative source of how to grow in and to live by grace. In Galatians 5:16-26, Paul refers to living by the Spirit, rather than by the law. Evidences of growing in grace and living by grace will appear in one's life as the fruit of the Spirit, identified by Paul as "love, joy, peace, patience, kindness, generosity, faithfulness, gentleness, self-control." Evidences of a lack of growth in grace and of the failure to live by grace will appear as the works of the flesh. Paul identifies these as "fornication, impurity, licentiousness, idolatry, sorcery, enmities, strife, jealousy, anger, quarrels, dissensions, factions, envy, drunkenness, carousing, and things like these." Paul makes the point that growing in grace and living by grace will make a list of prohibitions unnecessary. It is no accident that love heads Paul's list of the fruit of the Spirit. Earlier, Paul had said, "For the whole law is summed up in a single commandment, `You shall love your neighbor as yourself'" (Gal. 5:14; see also Rom. 13:8-10). The Christian lifestyle is determined by what self-giving love requires. Only in Scripture, in the revelation of God in the life, death, and resurrection of Jesus the Christ, can one find the full meaning of self-giving love.

Taking a somewhat different approach, Paul described the Christian life as having the "same mind . . . that was in Christ Jesus, who though he was in the form of God, . . . emptied himself, taking the form of a slave." (See Phil. 2:1-11.) The Christian lifestyle is one of serving others out of the motive of love. There can be no doubt that in no place other than in Scripture can one find the record of the servant ministry of Jesus the Messiah. Only in this record can one find the "infallible rule . . . of practice, the authoritative guide" for living as a servant of God, after the pattern of Jesus the servant Lord.

The Interpretation of Scripture

The Confession's most important statement concerning the interpretation of Scripture speaks about the centrality of the Christ event. It is a very direct statement. "God's word spoken in and through the scriptures should be understood in the light of the birth, life, death, and resurrection of Jesus of Nazareth" (1.04). A statement of Jesus himself is the basis for this affirmation of faith. To the scribes and Pharisees Jesus said, "You search the scriptures because you think that in them you have eternal life, and it is they that testify on my behalf" (Jn. 5:31). This statement is particularly significant when one remembers that the Scriptures to which Jesus referred comprised the Law (Torah) and the Prophets. This means that the Christian can and should read the Old Testament and indeed the whole Bible in light of the revelation of God in Jesus the Messiah.

In God's revelation, the focus is on the concept of God's word as the great Hebrew prophets developed this idea. The Gospel of John claims that the Word of God became flesh in Jesus Christ. This claim emphasizes that, in the most fundamental sense, the Bible is not the Word of God. Rather, the Bible functions as the authoritative witness to the living Word of God, who is Jesus the Messiah. Accordingly, the Confession does not refer to the Bible as the Word of God. It claims that God speaks the Word through the Bible whenever the community of faith interprets the Bible in light of the Word incarnate in Jesus the Christ. (See 1.06, 1.07).

A clue to what it means that all Scripture should be interpreted in light of the Christ event appears in another statement by Jesus himself. He said, "Do not think that I have come to abolish the law or the prophets [the Scriptures]; I have come not to abolish but to fulfill" (Mt. 5:17). The essence of what God was saying and doing in the events and teachings recorded in the Law and the Prophets appears "uniquely in Jesus Christ, the Word made flesh" (COF 1.02).

The report of an incident in John 8:1-11 clarifies the point. The scribes and Pharisees brought to Jesus a woman whom they said they had caught in adultery. The Law, in Leviticus 20:10 and Deuteronomy 22:22-24, says that a woman guilty of adultery shall be put to death. The scribes and Pharisees knew the Law, so they said, "In the law, Moses commanded us to stone such a woman." Instead of consenting to the clear demands of the Law, however, Jesus forgave the woman, and sent her away with the admonition to sin no more.

On the surface, it would appear that Jesus simply refused to obey the Law. In fact, what he did was to fulfill the Law. Matthew records a conversation between Jesus and a scribe about the greatest commandment. Jesus said that the greatest commandment was to love God with your whole being. He went on to say that the second greatest commandment was to love your neighbor as yourself. Actually, Jesus quoted from the Law, Deuteronomy 6:5 and Leviticus 19:18. He concluded his remarks with this revolutionary statement: "On these two commandments *hang all the law and the prophets.*" (See Mt. 22:34-40, italics added).

In acting with love, compassion and forgiveness toward the woman taken in adultery, Jesus fulfilled the Law and the Prophets. He demonstrated that the essence of their teachings occurs in the commandments to love God and persons. Paul showed a clear grasp of this revolutionary understanding of Scripture. In talking about how Christians should relate to each other and to unbelievers, Paul said, "Love does no wrong to a neighbor; therefore, love is the fulfilling of the law" (Rom 13:10).

This discussion of how Jesus dealt with the Law and Prophets of Scripture explains the affirmation in the Confession that "God's word spoken in and through scriptures should be understood in the light of the birth, life, death, and resurrection of Jesus of Nazareth" (COF 1.06). Interpreting Scripture in light of the Christ event involves understanding it in light of God's love, manifested in the covenant of grace. Jesus embodied the covenant of grace. Concerning the Christ event, the Gospel of John says, "From (Christ's) fullness we have all received, grace upon grace. The law indeed was given through Moses; grace and truth comes through Jesus Christ" (1:16-17).

The Study of Scripture

If one studies Scripture in light of the Christ event, in light of God's covenant of grace, the rest is methodology. The Confession of Faith does lay down one further precondition before dealing with methods of study: "In order to understand God's word spoken in and through the scriptures, persons must have the illumination of the Holy Spirit" (1.07). Actually, this affirmation follows the earlier affirmation that God inspired those who wrote the Scriptures. Inspiration is God-given insight into what God was saying and doing in the events of nature and history recorded in the Bible. This inspiration is critical because the meaning of the events was not apparent in the factual record. The illumination of the reader is, in some sense, the counterpart of the inspiration of the writer.

Paul understood this character of Scripture, especially when studied in light of the Christ event. This is how he explained the illumination of the Spirit to the Corinthian church: "No one comprehends what is truly God's [words and deeds] except the Spirit of God. Now we have received . . . the Spirit that is from God, so that we may understand the gifts bestowed on us by God" (1 Cor. 2:11-12). The only Scriptures that Paul ever read were the Law and the Prophets. From these Scriptures he preached the Good News of God's Word in Jesus the Messiah. It is ironic that this important precondition for the study of Scripture is at the same time a source of perversion and abuse. The history of the Christian church is filled with examples of persons who claimed to have a special inspiration concerning the meaning of a particular portion of Scripture. Many times this has led to controversy and division within the church. This is the reason that the Confession goes on to provide a methodology for the study of the Scriptures. The use of this methodology will help to guard against private interpretations (COF 1.07; 1 Pet. 1:2-21).

The methodology recommended by the Confession of Faith for Bible study begins with an inquiry into the historical setting of the particular book in which the text under consideration appears. The more one learns about the original historical setting of a book, the more one is able to get a feel for what the writer was saying to the first readers of the book. When one gets a grasp of the original historical circumstances, one is better able to understand what God was saying and doing in those circumstances. This kind of study will bear fruit in enabling persons to understand what God may be doing and saying in the circumstances of their own lives. Fortunately, many reliable helps are available to assist the serious Bible student in recreating the original historical setting. These include Bible dictionaries, encyclopedias, commentaries, and books on the history and geography of Bible times.

The second component of a good methodology of Bible study is to compare scripture with scripture. This process should begin with the immediate context of a passage. The most frequent violation of the meaning of Scripture occurs when readers attempt to interpret a verse or passage without regard for its immediate context. The larger context is the entire book in which the passage is found. A reader can understand this larger context only through an analysis of the contents of the book. An outline of the book based on an analysis of its contents is an important tool in the study of a particular portion of the book.

Only when one has dealt with both the immediate and the larger contexts of a text can one proceed in a meaningful way to compare the passage with passages on the same topic in other books of the Bible. A good concordance is helpful in this dimension of study. It is important, also, that one have some overall understanding of the main themes of the entire Bible. This will give coherence to the study, and will prevent it from becoming piecemeal in character. The Confession of Faith provides such an overall framework of themes for Bible study.

The other two steps which the Confession recommends will be particularly helpful in guarding against private interpretations. Students of the Bible should "listen to the witness of the church throughout the centuries, and share insights with others in the covenant community" (1.07). The study of the Bible, like its writing, should be an undertaking of the covenant community. People in the covenant community through the centuries have been studying the Bible. Sharing in the results of their study, through their writings, can be a rich experience. Group study within the fellowship of the church today is also a healthy corrective to tendencies toward private interpretations.

For Discussion

1. What are your initial reactions to the description of Scripture as a historical story into which is woven a testimony of faith about what God was doing and saying in the events reported? How does this view of Scripture compare with the tradition of telling stories within our families as a means of learning who we are and to whom we belong?
2. Do an exercise in Bible study, employing this view of Scripture. Read the account of Saul's conversion in Acts 9:1-22 or the story of David and Goliath from 1 Samuel 17. How might these stories have been told by an objective reporter? What has the community of faith added to the stories which enables them to communicate the message of faith? How is this approach to dealing with an event reported in Scripture similar to the way you deal with an event in your own experience?
3. What is your reaction to the statement that Scripture is not "an authority on every subject"? How does your response inform your attitude toward scientific knowledge? How does the Scripture help you deal with contemporary issues such as advances in genetic research, euthanasia, nuclear weapons, and/or feminism?
4. How have you used the Scriptures as an authority for Christian practice/living in your own life? How have you observed others make inappropriate use of the authority of Scripture?
5. How careful are you in every attempt to understand the meaning of a passage of Scripture, always to ask, "How is this to be understood in light of the birth, life, death and resurrection of Jesus of Nazareth? What does this say about your understanding of the Hebrew Scriptures we call the Old Testament?
6. What is your primary method of studying the Scripture? How does your practice compare with what is outlined in the Confession of Faith?
7. How does the Scripture become more meaningful within the context of the covenant community? What are some advantages of studying the Bible with others in the church as opposed to private study? Does your church offer adequate opportunities for group study of the Bible? Are you aware of resources to enhance your church's Bible study? Contact the Board of Christian Education for suggestions.

CHAPTER 3

GOD'S CREATION OF PERSONS: THEIR REBELLION

Read Confession of Faith 1.10-1.12, 2.01-2.06 and all Scriptures listed for these sections.

Introduction

The Confession of Faith says that God created persons. There is no reference to body or soul, simply to persons. This claim is consistent with the account in Genesis 1:27, which says, "So God created humankind [persons] in his image." The account in Genesis 2:7 says that persons are created of dust; and when God "breathed . . . the breath of life" into them, they became living beings (persons).

The Confession of Faith affirms, also, that "Among all forms of life, only human beings are created in God's image" (1.11). This affirmation concerning the nature of persons finds its basis in Genesis 1:26-27; 5:1-2; and 9:1-7. Though these passages speak of the image of God in persons, they do not explain what this means. In fact, the idea of the image is not specifically defined anywhere in Scripture. Like most biblical doctrines, it requires careful and prayerful reflection on the entire biblical record.

The Confession gives some direction to this process when it says, "To reflect the divine image is to worship, love and serve God" (1.11). In a somewhat different description of the creation of persons, the Confession says that in their creation "God . . . gives them the capacity and freedom to respond to divine grace in loving obedience" (2.01). Taken together, these statements seem to say that the nature of the divine image in persons exists in their relationship to God the Creator, and not in some inherent substance, quality, characteristic or ability which they possess. Finally, the Confession says that persons, who are created for a relationship of love and obedience toward God, "rebel against God, lose the right relationship with God, and become slaves to sin and death" (2.04). This is a reference to what is sometimes called original sin, or the fall. The fundamental alienation of persons from God affects who they are as persons, and disfigures the image of God in them.

What it means to be a person and what it means for a person to be created in the image of God deserve discussion. The rebellion of persons against God and the impact of this rebellion on persons, and on the image of God within them demands inquiry. The New Testament claims that the life and ministry of Jesus of Nazareth serves as humanity's best example of what it means to be a person, and to be a person created in the image of God. An examination of Jesus Christ, the second Adam, will clarify what it means that the first Adam, and all his descendants, are willfully disobedient and "inclined toward sin in all aspects of their being."

God Creates Persons

The Bible affirms both a kinship of persons to all living things and a uniqueness that distinguishes them from all other living things. The bond of kinship lies in the affirmation that God created all living things, including persons, from the ground—the dust of the earth. (See Gen. 2:7-8, 19.) The creation account seems to suggest that the uniqueness of persons, at least in part, comes from the fact that God breathed into these creatures of clay the breath of life, thereby constituting them as living beings. Despite the fact that the creation account makes no mention of body and soul, a common interpretation of these texts holds that a person is composed of two parts, a physical, mortal body, within which dwells a non-physical, immortal soul. This view persists both in theological writings and in popular theological understanding, in the face of clear evidence that it derives from Greek philosophy and not from Scripture.

The Greek view is that a person has a dual nature, body and soul. The body is regarded as essentially evil, the source of animal lusts. The only part of this dualistic person that has value is the immortal soul. The historical existence of a person is a time when the immortal soul lies imprisoned in an evil body. This view leads to a variety of lifestyles, ranging from severe discipline of the body in order to restrain its animal lusts, to neglect and abuse of the body, which is of no value, or to unbridled licentiousness involving what is ultimately a throw-away body.

The biblical view of a person recognizes the complex nature of this creature of dust into which God breathed the breath of life. This complexity centers, in part, in the inter-relationship of the physical and non-physical dimensions of the self. In fact, this complexity continues to puzzle modern science and psychology, as they seek to understand that dimension of the self that is more than the sum of its parts. One way to view the complex nature of a person is to say that this creature of dust is more than a physical being. Theologically, this *more than* is related both to what it means to be a person and to be in the image of God. The *more than* is not a reference to something in this creature of dust such as an immaterial soul. Rather, it is a reference to what this creature of dust becomes in relationship with God.

The Hebrew language of the Old Testament had no word to designate the body, in the Greek sense of that term. What the Greeks called the body the Hebrews regarded as an essential aspect of what it means to be a person. This led ultimately, in the Old Testament, to the affirmation that death is not the end of creatures of dust, into whom God breathed the breath of life. They will be resurrected in the final consummation of history. (See Dan. 12:2).

When scholars translated the Old Testament into the Greek language, a problem arose. Translators could not find terms in the Greek language which communicated the fundamental unity of the person. The Greek language had developed as the instrument of Greek thought, which made a radical distinction between the physical, mortal body and the non-physical, immortal soul. The translators had no alternative but to use the Greek terms, but they attempted to give them meanings that would communicate the concept of a person in the Old Testament sense. The original language of the New Testament was Greek. As was the case with the translators of the Old Testament into Greek, the New Testament writers used the Greek terms for body and soul, but they defined these terms to mean something different from what they usually meant in Greek philosophy. Failure to pay careful attention to this redefinition of terms by the New Testament writers has led to a widespread theological use of the terms body and soul in ways that reflect Greek philosophy rather than a biblical understanding. The persistence today of the use of these terms in ways that are alien to biblical thought testifies to the continuing influence of Greek philosophy in western culture. A careful study of the Pauline writings will show that Paul used the term flesh (body) to refer to the old self, which is in bondage to sin and death. By contrast, he used the term spirit (soul) to refer to the new self, which is born of the Spirit. (See Rom. 7:14–8:17; Gal. 5:16-26.) In no instance, when Paul does use the term body to refer to the physical dimension of the self, does he suggest that it is evil. The view that the physical body is fundamental to what it means to be a person, therefore essentially good, is at the heart of Paul's argument against prostitution in the Corinthian correspondence. At the conclusion of this argument he asks, "Or do you not know that your body is a temple of the Holy Spirit within you . . . ? For you were bought with a price; therefore glorify God in your body." (See 1 Cor. 6:12-20.)

At the same time, the New Testament clearly affirms that following death in this historical existence, the person who has been born of the Spirit will continue in fellowship with God, untroubled by the limitations and imperfections that prevail in the world. The language of the community of faith commonly says that such a person goes to heaven. However, the full redemption of this person is not complete until the resurrection of the body at the end of the age. Paul described this interim period between taking off the earthly tent and putting on the heavenly tent as being naked, without a body. (See 2 Cor. 5:1-5).

The effects of the destruction of the basic unity of the self do not constitute evidence that persons have an essentially dual nature. For now, this commentary will proceed further with an inquiry into what it means that this creature of clay, who is a person, is made in the image of God.

Persons in the Image of God

The initial text dealing with the image of God, Genesis 1:26, includes the statement that God gave persons dominion over the creation. This text suggests that one aspect of what it means for persons to be in the image of God is that they are in a relationship of responsibility toward God with regard to the rest of creation. The second creation account, Genesis 2:4-25, confirms this relationship of responsibility in this way: "The Lord God took the man and put him in the garden of Eden to till it and keep it" (v. 15). The responsibility of humankind continued when man was permitted to name the animals (vv. 19-20).

The Confession of Faith affirms this relationship of responsibility in this way: "Because of their God-given nature, persons are responsible for their choices and actions toward God, each other, and the world" (2.02). The Confession gives further definition of this responsibility to God as a stewardship of the natural world. "Its resources, beauty, and order are given in trust to all people, to care for, to conserve, to enjoy, to use for the welfare of all, and thereby to glorify God" (1.12).

Genesis 5:1-2 reaffirms the statement made in Genesis 1:26-27 concerning the creation of persons in the divine image. In Genesis 5:3, the scripture says of Adam, that "he became the father of a son in his likeness, according to his image, and named him Seth." The term translated image in 5:3 is the same term used in 5:1. This usage suggests that the likeness of persons to God is similar to family relationships, connections between children and parents. Therefore, the relationship of responsibility between humanity and God is comparable to the responsibility of a child to a parent. The fundamental sacredness of this parent-child (God-person) relationship is the reason that the killing of persons is the equivalent of an attack on God, "for in his own image God made humankind" (Gen. 9:6). The prophets reinforce understanding the image of God in persons in terms of family relationships when they describe the relationship of God to the covenant community. As the community called out and redeemed by God, Israel becomes God's child. God inspired Moses to say these words to Pharaoh: "'Israel is my first born son . . . . Let my son go that he may worship me'" (Ex. 4:22-23). Through the prophet Hosea, God said, "When Israel was a child, I loved him, and out of Egypt I called my son" (Hos. 11:1). Finally, speaking through Jeremiah about the covenant community in captivity in Babylon, God said, "I have been a father to Israel, and Ephraim is my first born" (Jer. 31:9). The use of the parent-child metaphor to describe the relationship of persons to God opens new dimensions in the meaning of the image of God in persons. Not only are persons responsible to God, as children to a parent, but they owe their very lives to God. They are bound to God by the grace (gift) of love, a covenant of grace, just as children are bound to their parents.

Indeed, the Confession says that the essence of what it means to be a person created in the divine image is "to [freely] respond to divine grace in loving obedience" (2.01). The Confession defines the essential freedom that belongs to the image of God in persons as the freedom to love. It is the freedom of personal relationships. This was the freedom that Adam and Eve exercised as they daily walked and talked with God "in the garden at the time of the evening breeze" (Gen 3:8). It is this freedom that sin caused humanity to lose.

When Moses spoke to the people of Israel as they prepared to enter the land of Canaan, he told them that the way of life was "loving the Lord your God, obeying him, and holding fast to him, for that means life to you . . ." (Deut. 30:20). Indeed, Jesus summed up the Law (Torah) and the Prophets in the commandments to love God and one's neighbor (Mt. 22:37-40.) In the Galatian letter, Paul defined Christian freedom as the freedom to love (See Gal 5:1-14.) The Confession affirms this definition of the primary freedom given to persons in their creation. Despite the insights the Scripture offers concerning the nature of the divine image in persons, certain limitations to this understanding exist. These limitations grow out of the fact that persons always exist under the conditions of sin, never as they were created by God to be. In the biblical story there is no significant segment of time, after the original creation, in which persons appear to be living as they were created to be, no time at which they are exercising the God-given "capacity and freedom to respond to divine grace in loving obedience" (COF 2.01). Reflecting on human history under the conditions of sin, Paul wrote: "For though (persons) knew God, they did not honor him as God or give thanks to him, but became futile in their thinking, and their senseless minds were darkened. Claiming to be wise [i.e. from eating the fruit of the tree of the knowledge of good and evil], they became fools, and they exchanged the glory of the immortal God for images resembling a mortal human being or birds or four footed animals or reptiles" (Rom 1:21-23).

The Rebellion of Persons

The Confession of Faith says, "As did Adam and Eve, all persons rebel against God [and] lose the right relationship with God" (2.04). In its essential nature, sin is not the transgression of law, for it is not a covenant of law that binds God to persons. Rather, sin is a violation of the covenant of grace, for it is a covenant of grace that binds persons to God. Sin is a violation of that essential relationship which constitutes the meaning of being in the image of God. It is in this sense that the image of God in persons is said to be disfigured because of original sin.

The divine-human relationship is personal, like that of a family. It follows, then, that sin is like the rebellion of a child. It is the rejection of the personal relationship of dependence and responsibility, the relationship of trust and love. Sin is the arrogant reach of persons for the fruit that promises to make finite human beings into gods. It is the ungrateful rejection of God, who alone is the source of life. A careful analysis of the account in Genesis of the original sin will reveal both the understanding of the personal character of the divine human relationship and the significance of the loss of that relationship (the image) because of sin. Both creation accounts suggest that the image of God in persons means a personal relationship between God and the creatures into whom God breathed the breath of life. God's personal communication with Adam and Eve immediately indicates this understanding.

In the first account, the claim that persons are created in the divine image immediately precedes a blessing and a command. "God blessed them, and God *said to them*, 'Be fruitful and multiply . . .'" (Gen. 1:27, italics added). The account continues, "God *said to them*, 'See I have given you every plant . . .'" (Gen 1:29, italics added). This reference to a relationship in which personal communication occurs is even more explicit in the second creation account. God warns man about the tree of knowledge. God promises him a helper as his partner, and enlists him in naming the animals (Gen. 2:15-20). More particularly, the picture drawn in Genesis 3:1-13 is of daily communication between God and Adam and Eve; God comes "walking in the garden at the time of the evening breeze." The suggestions seems to be that this was a regular event, a time of walking and talking together.

When the man and woman were nowhere to be found, God called out, "Where are you?" The daily fellowship had been disrupted by disobedience and rebellion. Instead of receiving life daily, as a gift from God (eating from the tree of life), the man and woman had eaten from the tree which the serpent said would make them gods.

From the divine side of this personal relationship, there was grace (love) in the daily gift of life, a desire for daily fellowship (worship), trust in the delegation of stewardship responsibility, and providential care in the warning about the limits of creaturehood. In their rebellion against God, the persons made in the divine image distrusted God, and refused to believe what God had told them about a certain tree in the garden. In their arrogance, they refused to recognize their limitations as finite creatures, and reached for a fruit they hoped would make them gods.

The forbidden fruit came from what was described as the tree of the knowledge of good and evil. One translation of the phrase knowledge of good and evil suggests that it is similar to the phrase from A to Z, or from top to bottom. One who knows everything from A to Z, or from top to bottom, knows everything. With such knowledge Adam and Eve intended to create their own self-centered world, in which they could be independent of God, in control of their own existence. In their rebellion they had confused and distorted being in the image of God to mean being gods.

In breaking their relationship with God, Adam and Eve lost the freedom to eat daily from the fruit of the tree of life. Death was not God's punishment for their sin. In eating the forbidden fruit they killed themselves, cutting themselves off from God, the source of life. An analogy from parent-child relationships may be helpful at this point. Parents do not say to their children, "If you drink that cup of poison, I will punish you by killing you." Rather, they say, "If you drink that cup of poison, you will die." Paul understood what had happened with Adam and Eve, when he wrote, "The *wages* of sin is death" (Rom. 6:23, italics added). Paul went on to describe this universal predicament of the human family, which followed this rebellion, as bondage to sin and death. (See Rom. 5:12-14).

The Genesis story emphasizes the rebellion of persons against God and the loss of daily fellowship with God in the account of their expulsion from the garden (Gen. 3:22-24). The existence which remains for persons who declare their independence from God is one filled with sorrow and trouble. The family, which was a blessing from God, became a source of pain, jealousy, and strife. Because of sin, stewardship responsibility for the earth became at times an onerous task, and at other times a pursuit of unbridled self interests. Gen. 3:13–4:12).

The impact of sin on the relationship of persons to God (on the image of God in persons), affects the most basic level of the unity of the self. The well-known psychiatrist Karl Menninger wrote a book entitled *Man Against Himself*, in which he described the kind of internal war that rages within an individual.

Paul himself had experienced such a war when he wrote, "So I find it to be a law that when I want to do good, evil lies close at hand. For I delight in the law of God in my inmost self, but I see in my members another law at war with the law of my mind, making me captive to the law of sin that dwells in my members. Wretched man that I am! Who will rescue me from this body of death?" (Rom. 7:21-24). This basic disunity of the self is not finally overcome until the resurrection of the body at the end of the age.

The Confession puts it this way: "In willfully sinning all people become guilty before God and under divine wrath" (2.05). The gravity of the human predicament is overwhelming. It is not the case that persons are simply liable to die and go to hell. Rather, it is that all persons are already *dead in trespasses and sin*, already in bondage to sin and death (hell).

This predicament is what theologians have called original sin. The Confession describes the original sin of persons as being "inclined toward sin in all aspects of their being" (2.03). In ordinary language, this inclination is the tendency to self-centeredness. It is not an explicit sinful act, but a disposition out of which all sinful acts arise.

Original sin is not something transmitted in the genes from one generation to the next, reaching all the way back to the first parents. The Confession describes it this way: "As did Adam and Eve, all persons rebel against God" (2.04). In the words of Paul, "Therefore, just as sin came into the world through one man, and death through sin, so death spread to all, *because all have sinned*" (Rom. 5:12, italics added). The universality of original sin not only describes the complicity of all persons in this condition; it also suggests the pervasive consequence of sin for the whole creation. The Confession affirms this truth in this way: "The alienation of persons from God affects the rest of creation, so that the whole creation stands in need of God's redemption" (2.02). The growing ecological crisis in the world today is dramatic confirmation of how the ignorance and selfishness (sinfulness) of persons have affected the natural order.

Again, Paul's insight into the nature and consequences of original sin reflects his understanding of what he described as the futility of the creation because of its "bondage to decay (death)" (Rom. 8:20-21). Earlier the prophets had identified idolatry, war, disease, hunger, injustice, and even hostility among animals as evidences of the universal problem of sin and rebellion against God. (See Am. 8:1-14; Hos. 4:1-3; Isa. 24:1-20; Joel 3:9-15). As Paul puts it, "The whole creation has been groaning in travail together until now," waiting for God's redemption (Rom. 8:22, RSV).

The Second Adam

It is difficult, if not impossible, under the conditions of original sin, to identify and describe the true nature of what Scripture calls the image of God in persons. At this point, it is helpful to recall a basic principle of biblical interpretation, emphasized in the Confession of Faith: "God's word spoken in and through the scriptures should be understood in light of the birth, life, death, and resurrection of Jesus of Nazareth" (1.06). This includes what Scripture says about the image of God in persons. In accordance with this principle, a look at Jesus of Nazareth will reveal what the Scripture means concerning the image of God in persons. Because of the magnitude of the problem of sin, the restoration of the image of God in persons, and the redemption of the whole creation require nothing less than the living, suffering, loving presence in the world of the great God of the universe. Jesus of Nazareth, whom the apostle Paul called the second Adam, uniquely manifested this Presence. (See Rom. 5:12-14; 1 Cor. 15:45-49.) It was in the second Adam that God disclosed the true image of God in persons.

The Gospel of John states, "No one has ever seen God. It is God the only Son, who is close to the Father's heart, who has made him known" (1:18). Throughout his ministry, Jesus stressed his unity with God the Father. During the time he met with the Twelve, immediately before his crucifixion, Jesus said, "If you know me, you will know my Father also. From now on *you do know him and you have seen him*" (Jn. 14:7, italics added). When Philip, and perhaps others, failed to understand, Jesus said simply, "Whoever has seen me has seen the Father. . . . The words that I say to you I do not speak on my own; but the Father who dwells in me does his works" (Jn. 14:9, 10). Jesus of Nazareth lived as persons were created to be, reflecting the perfect image and likeness of God the Father.

Indeed, the Gospel of John begins with the affirmation that God is incarnate in Jesus of Nazareth. The Word who was God "became flesh and lived among us, and we have seen his glory, the glory of the Father's only son, full of grace and truth" (Jn. 1:14). It is not surprising, then, that Paul spoke of "the gospel of the glory of Christ, *who is the image of God*" (2 Cor. 4:4, italics added). However, in contrast to the first Adam, who brought the death of sin into the world, "the last Adam [Jesus Christ] became a life giving spirit" (1 Cor. 15:45). Finally, in Colossians 1:15, Jesus the Messiah is identified as "the image of the invisible God, the first born of all creation."

The inescapable conclusion from this inquiry is that to truly know Jesus of Nazareth and his relationship to God the Father is to know what it means to be created in the image of God. It is to live in a relationship of complete harmony with God the Father, like the relationship of a loving, obedient, responsible child to a parent. As the Gospel of John emphasizes, however, such knowledge is not obtained in the ordinary manner of knowing. "He [Jesus] was in the world, and the world came into being through him, yet the world did not know him. . . But to all who received him, who believed in his name, he gave power to become the children of God" (Jn. 1:10). The children of God! Created in the image of God!

Children of the first Adam find themselves created anew in the likeness of the second Adam, Jesus the Christ. This is the hope and promise of God's covenant of grace with the human family.

For Discussion

1. This chapter claims that the view of a person as being composed of a mortal body and an immortal soul is an idea from Greek philosophy rather than Scripture. How do you react to this claim?
2. What has been your understanding of the image of God in persons? How does your own life and the lives of others close to you reflect the image of God?
3. Cite examples of how our culture reinforces our tendency to regard "the body" as the source of evil impulses.
4. What has been your understanding of the doctrine of original sin (the inclination to sin)? How seriously is this doctrine taken in the church today? How does a clear understanding of original sin make possible a greater appreciation for God's grace?
5. What do you understand to be the meaning and significance of the phrase "in bondage to sin and death"?
6. In light of your reading of this chapter, reflect on the following statements:

   "When I die I won't really die, I'll just pass on."

   "My body is finite; my soul is immortal."

CHAPTER 4

GOD'S COVENANT OF GRACE

Read Confession of Faith, 3.01-3.04 and Scriptures listed for these sections.

Introduction

The dominant theological theme of the 1984 Confession of Faith is the covenant of grace. The term covenant appears forty-one times in the 1984 Confession of Faith, and covenant of grace appears seven times. In fourteen instances covenant identifies the church as the covenant community, the community of people saved by and living under the rule of Jesus the Messiah. Every doctrine in the Confession appears in the context of the covenant of grace, which is always described as a personal relationship established freely and unconditionally by God with the human family.

In order fully to understand the audacity and creativity of Cumberland Presbyterian theology in the latter part of the 20th century with its making the covenant of grace central to its interpretation of Scripture, one needs some perspective on the theological journey of the church since 1810.

The primary motive for establishing the Cumberland Presbyterian Church was to give persons the theological freedom and understanding to proclaim to all people the good news of God's grace in Jesus Christ. Evidence that the 1984 Confession of Faith is faithful to that motive appears in the first paragraph of the Introduction, which cites John 3:16 as "the statement of purpose of this Confession of Faith and its organizing principle." In the 1984 Confession of Faith, this evangelical tradition plants its theological roots in God's covenant of grace.

Developments in Covenant Theology

In 1810 the creedal statement of the Presbyterian Church in the U.S.A. was the Westminster Confession. With certain exceptions, the Cumberland Presbyterian Church adopted this confession as its creedal statement. The Westminster Confession embodied a covenant theology, but it was a theology of two covenants, a covenant of works (law) and a covenant of grace. Two covenant theology had been the dominant theology of Presbyterian and Reformed churches since the late 16th and early 17th centuries.

The Westminster Confession says, "The first covenant [God] made with man was a covenant of works, wherein life was promised to Adam, and in him to his posterity, upon condition of perfect and personal obedience" (WC 7.2). The negative component of the covenant of law (works), was the threat of punishment by death if the terms of the covenant were not met. The original relationship that God established with the human family was legal in nature. The legal character of this relationship determined the nature of human sin, God's redemption in Jesus Christ, and the Christian life. The claim was that, in all respects, God dealt with persons in terms of law, with its motives of reward for obedience and punishment for disobedience.

The Westminster Confession goes on to say that Adam violated the covenant of works, placing himself and his posterity under the penalty of death. At this point, "the Lord was pleased to make a second (covenant), commonly called the covenant of grace: wherein he freely offers unto sinners life and salvation by Jesus Christ." (WC 7.3). It is not the case, however, that the second covenant replaced the first covenant. The covenant of works remained in force. According to the Westminster Confession, the covenant of grace was simply an expedient that enabled persons, by way of Jesus Christ, to satisfy the conditions of the covenant of works. In this system, salvation became a legal transaction. The Westminster Confession describes the situation in this manner: Because of the sin of Adam, all of his descendants stood before the judgment bar of God under penalty of death. Jesus Christ offered himself as a legal substitute to satisfy the penalty of death required by the covenant of law or works. Actually, Jesus Christ satisfied the terms of the covenant of law in two ways. First, during his earthly life, Jesus Christ obeyed the law perfectly. The merits of this perfect obedience became a substitute for the disobedience of Adam and his posterity. Second, in his death on the cross, Jesus suffered the legal penalty for the disobedience of Adam and his posterity, thus satisfying God's demand for justice before the law. (See WC 8.5.) At this point, the logic of the Westminster Confession breaks down. The sin of Adam made all his descendants guilty, and placed them under the penalty of death. By contrast, the righteousness of Jesus Christ, the second Adam, and his satisfaction of the penalty of the law through his death, benefitted only the elect. According to the Westminster Confession, before the foundation of the world, God had decreed that "some men and angels are predestined unto everlasting life, and others to everlasting death" (WC 6.3).

Cumberland Presbyterians rejected the doctrines of predestination and limited atonement, believing that they were not clearly supported by Scripture. This theological change set Cumberland Presbyterians free to affirm, without reservation, that "God so loved the world that he gave his only Son, so that everyone who believes in him may not perish but may have eternal life" (Jn. 3:16). Thus within the Presbyterian and Reformed tradition, it was Cumberland Presbyterians who proclaimed an unqualified Gospel, Good News to all people.

In 1814 the Cumberland Presbyterian Church adopted a revision of the Westminster Confession which deleted the doctrines of predestination and limited atonement. However, the 1814 Confession left the two covenant framework intact. The covenant of works remained primary, and the covenant of grace secondary. The Confession defined the divine human relationship in terms of law rather than grace. God was the law giver and the stern judge who enforced the law.

By the middle of the 19th century persons in the Cumberland Presbyterian Church began saying that the 1814 revision of the Westminster Confession did not fully represent what Cumberland Presbyterians believed to be the essential teachings of the Bible. By 1883 this concern led to a further revision of the Confession of Faith. Among other changes, this new revision began to move away from the two covenant theology of the Westminster Confession and of the 1814 Cumberland Presbyterian revision. References to the covenant of works and some of the legal language that reflect this covenant still remained in the 1883 revision. (See 1883 COF, 22, 23, 30, 49.) There were, however, two significant modifications affecting the nature of the covenant of works. First, in its ultimate form, the law of that covenant was defined in terms of Jesus' summary given of it in Mark 12:3-31. A definition of the law as a command to love suggests that the relationship between God and persons was personal rather than legal. (See 1883 COF, 66-68.) Second, the penalties of the law are the natural consequences rather than the judicial punishment for sin. That is, death is not God's judicial punishment for sin, but is sin's natural consequences.

One other significant change in the 1883 Confession suggests that the covenant of works was no longer the controlling theological concept for all doctrine. In reference to the work of Jesus Christ as Savior, the 1814 Confession followed the Westminster Confession, saying, "The Lord Jesus, by his perfect obedience and sacrifice of himself, . . . fully satisfied the justice of his Father," as the law required (1814 COF, 8.4). The 1883 Confession of Faith describes the work of salvation in Jesus Christ as propitiation rather than satisfaction. (See 1883 COF, 31.) Jesus becomes "the propitiation for the sins of the world," rather than the one who has "satisfied the justice of his Father."

Propitiation refers to an action accomplished to restore a personal relationship, not an action designed to satisfy the penalty of law. It presupposes a disposition to understand the divine-human relationship in personal rather than legal terms. A study of the writings of Stanford G. Burney, Professor of Theology at Cumberland University, and chairperson of the 1883 revision committee, confirms this understanding of the term propitiation in the 1883 Confession.

In *Atonement and Law Reviewed,* Burney explicitly rejected the claim that the basic relationship which God established with the human family was a legal one. He argued that it is more properly understood as personal, like that of a father to his children. Accordingly, he defined sin as breaking or violating a personal relationship, rather than breaking a law. He argued that restoration of a personal relationship and not the satisfaction of a legal penalty accomplishes salvation. Burney used the term propitiation to describe the work of Christ in this restoration of the divine-human relationship.

Though the 1883 Confession marked the beginning of a movement away from the classical two covenant theology of the Westminster Confession, references to both a covenant of works and a covenant of grace persisted in Cumberland Presbyterian theology. The usual justification of a two covenant theology, however, became very different from that given in the Westminster Confession and the 1814 Cumberland Presbyterian Confession. This new justification for a two covenant theology held that during the period of the Old Testament the religion of law prevailed, but the coming of Christ replaced the religion of law with a religion of grace. This religion of grace appears in the New Testament.

The Westminster Confession and all three Cumberland Presbyterian Confessions explicitly reject the view that the Old Testament teaches a religion of law and the New Testament a religion of grace. In classical two covenant theology, only Adam and Eve had been bound initially and solely by the covenant of law, and this only before they sinned. After their sin, the covenant of grace became operative as an expedient to satisfy the conditions of the covenant of law. Accordingly, the Westminster Confession of Faith and all three Cumberland Presbyterian Confessions of Faith say that the laws, signs, prophesies, sacrifices, etc., contained in the Old Testament are vehicles of the covenant of grace, later manifested fully in Jesus Christ. (See WC, 7.50; 1814 CPC, 7.5; 1883 CPC, 24; 1984 CPC, 3.04.)

The one covenant of grace contains elements of what many call the old and the new covenants. An explanation of the old and the new in one covenant will emerge with an exploration of the nature of the covenant of grace. The 1984 Cumberland Presbyterian Confession sets forth the biblical basis for the one covenant, the covenant of grace.

Understanding the covenant of grace requires beginning in the New Testament, in keeping with the general principle of Bible study laid down in the 1984 Confession of Faith: that all Scripture be read and "understood in light of the birth, life, death, and resurrection of Jesus of Nazareth," (COF, 1.06). An appropriate beginning point is Paul's interpretation of the Christ event, which he derived from the Law and the Prophets, the only Scriptures he knew.

In the Galatian letter Paul wrote, "We know that a person is justified not by works of the law (a covenant of law), but through faith in Jesus Christ (a covenant of grace)" (Gal. 2:16). He also claimed that this had always been the case, showing that God's covenant with Abraham, a covenant of grace, had come 430 years before God gave the Law at Sinai. (See Gen. 12:1-3; 17:1-8; Gal. 3:1-18.) There are indications of God's covenant of grace as early as the creation story in Genesis. This is the reason that the Confession of Faith, before it deals with the creation, affirms that "by word and action God invites persons into a covenant relationship" (1.03). The Confession goes on to say, "God's covenant is a relationship of grace. It appears in various forms and manifestations in scripture but always as one of grace" (3.03).

The Prophetic Witness to the Covenant of Grace

The Confession says that the covenant relationship God established with people is of the nature of the family (3.02). The first prophet to use the metaphor of family life to describe the covenant relationship was Hosea. (See Hos. 2:16-20). The remarkable thing about Hosea's use of the metaphor of marriage to represent the covenant of grace was that he worked out of a tragic experience in his own marriage. His wife was unfaithful in the marriage relationship, and Hosea was inclined to deal with her in accordance with the law, to divorce her. (See Deut. 24:1.) The law provided, also, that an adulteress was to be stoned to death. (Lev. 20:10). As Hosea wrestled with his personal tragedy, he heard God say, "Go love a woman who has a lover and is an adulteress, just as the Lord loves the people of Israel" (Hos. 3:1).

Hosea's dealing with his unfaithful wife with grace rather than law raised that relationship above the level of a legal contract to the level of a personal covenant of love. In the process, Hosea learned that God's relationship to the covenant community was one of love, not law. Accordingly, Hosea described sin as adultery. It is not simply a violation of law, but an act of unfaithfulness in the most intimate, sacred personal relationship. It is a violation of the bond of love.

The prophets Isaiah, Jeremiah, and Ezekiel followed Hosea's use of the metaphor of marriage to describe the relationship of God to the covenant community. In the view of these prophets the marriage of God to the covenant community was marred by Israel's unfaithfulness. The description in Ezekiel 16:15 is typical of Israel's behavior. "But you trusted in your beauty, and played the whore because of your fame, and lavished your whorings on any passer-by." In response to such arrogance, God acted both with discipline and redemption. "Thus says the Lord God: `I will deal with you as you have done, you who have despised the oath, breaking the covenant; yet I will remember my covenant with you as in the days of your youth, and I will establish with you an everlasting covenant'" (Ez. 16:59).

The Old Testament prophets were primary interpreters of the covenant of grace in which God related to the covenant community. They made it clear that the community was not to understand this relationship in terms of ethnic exclusiveness. From the time of Abraham, God's covenant of grace provided that through the group called Israel, "all the families of the earth shall be blessed" (Gen. 12:3). Indeed, as Paul would later show, it was always God's purpose that Israel should be defined as a community of faith rather than as a particular ethnic group. He wrote, "So, you see, *those who believe* are descendants of Abraham" (Gal. 3:7, italics added). In an even more direct manner, Paul said, "For a person is not a Jew (Hebrew) who is one outwardly, nor is true circumcision something external and physical. Rather, a person is a Jew who is one inwardly" (Rom. 2:28-29).

In a little-noticed passage in the book of Amos, the prophet said that in God's sight there were no essential differences between Israelites and Ethiopians. Adding insult to injury, Amos went on to claim that God had guided the destinies of the Philistines and Syrians just as God had guided the Israelites. (See Am. 9:7). A vision of the messianic age found in Isaiah 19:19-25 presents God saying, "Blessed be Egypt my people, Assyria the work of my hands, and Israel my heritage." Given this recurring message in the Old Testament, it is not surprising that the book of Jonah presents God's sending a Hebrew evangelist named Jonah to preach in the city of Nineveh. The irony of this story is rich and significant. Nineveh was the capital of Assyria. 2 Kings 14:25 identifies Jonah as a resident of Northern Israel during the reign of Jeroboam II, a few years before Assyria conquered Northern Israel. In this context, the book of Jonah is clear evidence that God's will and purpose for the covenant community was that all nations be included in the covenant of grace. This is also the thrust of the vision in Isaiah 2:2-4, which states, "all nations shall stream" to the "mountain of the Lord's house" to learn the ways of the Lord, and to "walk in his paths."

Based on the writings of the Prophets, two things become clear about the covenant relationship into which the Confession of Faith says God invites persons. First, in the use of the metaphor of the marriage relationship, the prophets understood the covenant relationship as personal rather than legal, a covenant of love rather than of law. Second, the great prophets attacked the arrogance of ethnic Jews who tried to claim that they alone comprised the covenant community. Surprising as it may seem, the covenant of grace appears also in the Torah (Law).

The Covenant of Grace in the Torah

Genesis, the first book of the Law, shows that from the time of Abraham God acted toward Israel in accordance with the covenant of grace. It is understandable, then, that the second book of the Law, Exodus, shows God renewing a covenant with Israel that had been made originally with Abraham. (See Ex. 2:23-25.) The renewal of this covenant is set in the context of that glorious event in which, by grace, God delivered Israel delivered from bondage into freedom. After the exodus, Moses spoke these words from God: "You have seen what I did to the Egyptians, and how I bore you on eagles' wings and brought you to myself" (Ex. 19:4). This is testimony to the covenant of grace.

Classical covenant theology summarized the covenant of law in the Ten Commandments, which God gave at Sinai soon after the exodus. Two things about the Ten Commandments, however, deserve attention. First, the commandments are not stated in the usual form of laws, including the necessary sanctions—a promise of reward for obedience and a threat of punishment for disobedience. The Ten Commandments do not, as the Westminster Confession claims concerning the covenant of works, promise eternal life "upon condition of perfect and personal obedience." Indeed, only the fifth commandment contains any sort of promise for its obedience—long life for honoring parents. None of the commandments carries a threat of death for disobedience.

The second thing to note is the preface to the Ten Commandments which issues a call to remember God's gracious act of salvation in the exodus event: "I am the Lord your God, who brought you out of the land of Egypt, out of the house of slavery" (Ex. 20:2). The motive for observing the commandments that followed is clearly thanksgiving for redemption from bondage in Egypt. The content of the Ten Commandments is largely a negative description of what should be a grateful response of a people saved by the grace of God. If the Ten Commandments suggest anything concerning a covenant, they point to a prior covenant of grace, by which Israel had been saved.

A closer examination of the Genesis account of the relationship between God and the first persons fails to support the claim that this relationship was of the nature of a covenant of law (works). God did not say to Adam and Eve, "If you refrain from eating the fruit of the tree of the knowledge of good and evil, I will reward you with eternal life; but if you eat of that fruit, I will put you to death." Such a statement would have been the formula for a covenant of law (works). On the contrary, God laid down an unconditional command, like the commands of the Ten Commandments. "Of the tree of the knowledge of good and evil you shall not eat" (Gen. 2:17). God did warn them of the consequences of disobedience, but these consequences were not God's punishment. In effect, Adam and Eve killed themselves. The command in Genesis was not the promulgation of a covenant of law (works). It was the expression of love by a loving Parent, trying to teach children the limits of their finite existence.

The Law also includes indications that God did not intend the covenant community to be restricted to ethnic Jews. Commandments which provide for just actions toward aliens occur throughout the Torah. These statements are often tied to a remembrance that Israel was at one time itself an alien in a hostile land. An example appears in Exodus 23:9: "You shall not oppress a resident alien; you know the heart of an alien, for you were aliens in the land of Egypt." A commandment in Leviticus is even more remarkable: "The alien who resides among you shall be to you as a citizen among you; you shall love the alien as yourself, for you were aliens in the land of Egypt: I am the lord your God" (Lev. 19:34). In going beyond justice to love, God opens the way for aliens to share with Israelites in the worship of the God of the covenant. "An alien who lives with you, or who takes up permanent residence among you, and wishes to offer an offering . . . shall do so. . . . You and the alien shall be alike before the Lord" (Num. 15:14-15). The provisions in the Law which opened the Passover celebration to aliens are most surprising. The Passover was the central celebration of the covenant of grace—a remembrance of God's salvation of Israel. "Any alien residing among you who wishes to keep the passover to the Lord shall do so according to the statute of the passover; . . . you shall have one statute for both the resident alien and the native (Hebrew). (Num. 9:14). None of the commandments concerning aliens required that aliens become Hebrews, as in submission to the rite of circumcision.

The Ten Commandments and other laws which followed, did not constitute a covenant of works (law). They comprised a description of the kind of behavior appropriate for a people who were bound to God in a covenant of grace.

Indeed, Deuteronomy used the parent-child metaphor to describe the way in which God deals with persons and how they should respond. "Know then in your heart that as a parent disciplines a child so the Lord your God disciplines you. Therefore keep the commandments of the Lord your God, by walking in his way and by fearing him" (Deut. 8:5). It is not surprising, then, that as the Israelites were poised to go into Palestine, Moses talked to them about "loving the Lord your God, walking in all his ways, and holding fast to him" (Deut. 11:22). Even in the Law (Torah), the relationship of God to the human family finds expression in personal rather than in legal terms.

The New Testament and the Covenant of Grace

Writing to the congregation at Corinth, which included both Jews and Gentiles, Paul said of many Jewish religious leaders: "To this very day whenever Moses (the Torah) is read, a veil lies over their minds; but when one turns to the Lord (Jesus the Christ), the veil is removed" (2 Cor. 3:15). Taking the veil off the Law and the Prophets is exactly what the 1984 Confession of Faith attempts to do, when it urges that all Scripture be read in light of the Christ event. Reading the Scripture in light of the Christ event makes clear what the Confession of Faith affirms: "God's covenant is a relationship of grace. It appears in various forms and manifestations in the scriptures but always as one of grace" (3.03).

Two statements of Jesus serve as keys to any effort to understand the Old Testament "in light of the birth, life, death and resurrection of Jesus of Nazareth." First, in his attempt to set the scribes and Pharisees free from their erroneous views of the Law and the Prophets, Jesus said, "You search the scriptures because you think that in them you have eternal life, and it is they that testify on my behalf" (Jn. 5:39). Second, in the body of teachings in Matthew 5-7, Jesus said, "Do not think I have come to abolish the law or the prophets; I have come not to abolish but to fulfill" (Mt. 5:17). The claim that the Old Testament testifies concerning

Jesus the Messiah means simply that it testifies concerning God's covenant of grace. The claim that Jesus the Messiah fulfilled the Old Testament means simply that what is partial in the Old Testament concerning the covenant of grace was made complete in God's revelation in Jesus the Christ, to which the New Testament witnesses. Hebrews 1:1-3 confirms this understanding when it states, "Long ago God spoke to our ancestors in many and various ways by the prophets, but in these last days has spoken to us by a Son. . . . He is the reflection of God's glory and the exact imprint of God's very being."

The Word spoken in the Law and the Prophets was the same Word spoken in Christ—the Word of God's covenant of grace. The difference was in God's sending the Word of the covenant by a messenger, and speaking the Word in person in Jesus Christ. What many call the old covenant refers to the covenant of grace originally announced through messengers. This medium did not reveal the full scope of the covenant. What some call the new covenant refers to the covenant of grace fully manifested in Jesus Christ.

The Confession affirms that in both the Old Testament (Covenant) and the New Testament (Covenant), the Word of God speaks of only one covenant of grace in Jesus Christ. "Before Christ's coming, it [the one covenant of grace] was made effective by promises, prophesies, sacrifices, circumcision, the passover lamb, and other signs and ordinances delivered to the people of Israel" (3.04). The Confession continues: "Since Christ's coming, . . . the gospel of the covenant of grace is set forth simply and *yet in fullness and with spiritual power*" (3.05, italics added). The entire book of Hebrews presents a comparison of the old, partial revelation of the covenant of grace (the priesthood and the system of offerings and sacrifices provided for in the Torah) with the fullness of God's revelation of the covenant of grace in Jesus Christ. The writer of Hebrews puts it this way: "Jesus has now obtained a more excellent ministry, and to that degree he is the mediator of a better covenant, which has been enacted through better promises. For if the first covenant had been faultless, there would have been no need to look for a second one" (8:6-7).

The first or old covenant and the second or new covenant are not references to two different covenants. In fact, when the author of Hebrews compares the old and the new, he shows that they function in the same way, as covenants of grace. The old was somewhat faulty or partial and became obsolete because its medium (perishable sacrifices and offerings) was limited. The new is faultless, because the medium was none other than Jesus the Christ, "the reflection of God's glory and the exact imprint of God's very being" (Hebrews 1:3). The same letter later affirms, "The law (Torah) has only a shadow of the good things to come, not the true form of these realities" (Heb. 10:1).

For Discussion

1. What are your reactions to the claim that there is no biblical basis for the view that a covenant of works (law) was the original covenant of God with the human family?
2. What evidence do you see in the church, the world, and in your own life that many still believe in a covenant of works? What experience have you had with individuals who appear to believe that salvation comes by keeping laws or doing particular works?
3. Review the historical development of the movement of the Cumberland Presbyterian Church from a two covenant theology (law and grace) to a one covenant theology (grace alone). How does your own congregation manifest this doctrinal position? What happens in the life and work of your church which identifies it somewhere along the continuum between two covenants and one?
4. How does your familiarity with the view that the Old Testament teaches a religion of works and the New Testament a religion of grace color your theology?
5. How do you react to the view in Hebrews that the difference in the "old" and "new" covenants is a difference in degree (one partial and the other complete), rather than a difference in kind (law vs. grace)?

CHAPTER 5

GOD'S COVENANT IN CHRIST

Read Confession of Faith 3.05-3.11 and Scriptures listed for these sections.

Introduction

The Confession instructs persons to study all Scripture "in light of the birth, life, death and resurrection of Jesus of Nazareth" who is the "ultimate and supreme expression" of God's covenant of grace. Accordingly, following the direction of the apostle Paul in 2 Corinthians 3:15, the veil is no longer covering the Law (Torah) and the Prophets, and believers now understand these Scriptures in light of God's word in Jesus Christ.

The New Testament testifies to God's covenant of grace. The death of Christ alone, or the death and resurrection of Christ, sufficiently bear witness to God's covenant. The entire Gospel—the Good News of all that God has done and continues to do in the birth, life, death and resurrection of Jesus the Christ--displays the covenant of grace.

In the Birth and Life of Christ

The story of the birth of Jesus the Messiah testifies to the claim in the Old Testament that God's covenant relationship with the human family is personal in nature, like family relationships. God determined to relate to the human family by becoming incarnate in a person, Jesus of Nazareth. In this astounding event—the birth of a baby into the humble family of a carpenter—all the references in the Old Testament which describe God's relationship to persons in family terms find fulfillment. This intensely personal family event manifests the full meaning of God's covenant of grace.

In her song of joy concerning her pregnancy, Mary connected this family event with what God had been saying and doing for centuries in the covenant community. It was, she said, "in remembrance of his (God's) mercy (grace), according to the promise he made to our ancestors, to Abraham and to his descendants forever" (Lu. 1:54-55). God embodies the covenant of grace in the birth of a particular child to a particular family in a particular place at a particular time. Nevertheless, the event had universal significance. The Confession of Faith affirms: "God's work of reconciliation in Jesus Christ occurred at a particular time and place. Yet its powers and benefits extend to the believer *in all ages from the beginning of the world"* (3:11, italics added). When Simeon saw the Christ child, he said to God, "My eyes have seen your salvation, . . . a light for revelation to the Gentiles and for glory to your people Israel" (Lu. 2:30-32).

In his ministry, through word and deed, Jesus of Nazareth affirmed that God's covenant with the human family was and always has been personal, a covenant of grace. This thrust of his teachings disturbed then angered many of the scribes and Pharisees, who taught and practiced a religion based on a covenant of law. Jesus, however, did not regard his teachings as something different from what the Scriptures—the Law (Torah) and the Prophets—contained. Jesus said explicitly that what he taught was the fulfillment of the Law and the Prophets.

Two parables represent the teachings of Jesus concerning God's personal covenant of grace and illustrate his statement about the full meaning of the Law and the Prophets. Each begins with a person alienated from God. Each shows that God deals with sinners with grace to accomplish reconciliation. In the process, each parable explicitly rejects the claim that God is bound to persons and deals with them in terms of law. Jesus told the parable of the Pharisee and the tax collector in the context of a conversation with "some who trusted themselves that they were righteous." (See Lu. 18:9-14). This is an obvious reference to those scribes and Pharisees who understood that they were bound to God in a covenant of law, a covenant in which one earns favor with God (salvation) by faithful observance of the law.

The parable demonstrates two aspects of the situation of the Pharisee. First, he gave no indication of any sensitivity to a tendency to sin, nor to any feelings of guilt for past sins. Second, based on his scrupulous observance of the law, he was confident in his relationship with God. By contrast, the tax collector readily acknowledged his sinfulness, and he knew that his only hope was in the grace of God. The fact that he cried out for mercy indicates that he had some understanding, or at least some hope, that God dealt with sinners in terms of grace. It is clear that the parable contrasts two views of how God may be related to and deal with persons—according to law or grace. The thrust of the parable is to affirm that God deals with persons according to the covenant of grace.

The other parable, which is usually called the parable of the prodigal son, might more properly be called the parable of the gracious father. The first important thing to note about this parable is that it is set in the context of family life. The personal relationships within the family provide insights into the way the father (God) deals with his sons (persons).

The younger son made an unexpected and unusual demand for his inheritance, followed by an equally surprising decision to go into a far country. The parable pictures him as a self-centered, rebellious person, a young man who renounced his family. Later, though he was in the most desperate of circumstances, he did not expect ever to be received back into the family. He assumed that he would be dealt with according to law. At best, he might be employed as a servant.

In his return, the son had given no consideration to asking for forgiveness and restoration to the family. Then the miracle of grace occurred. Even before the son could ask for employment as a servant, the father welcomed him home as a son! The father gave no reprimand, nor did he lay down conditions for the return of the wayward son. Rather, he embraced his son, put a ring on his finger signifying his restoration to the family, and ordered a banquet to celebrate what the father called the resurrection of a dead son.

Clearly the personal bond reflected in the actions of the father was of the nature of the covenant of grace. This contrasts with the apparent assumption of the younger son, that he would be dealt with according to law. He knew that his conduct normally would have destroyed all family ties. Clearly the older son understood the family bond to be one of law. Under a covenant of law, the most severe of all punishments would have been imposed on such a rebellious son. The older son resented the unconditional act of forgiveness, the grace, which the father demonstrated. In his view, the least the father should have done would have been to require full restitution of the wasted inheritance and a period of harsh probation for the younger son as prerequisites for his restoration to the family.

Even when Jesus referred directly to the teachings of the Law (Torah), he set them in the context of a covenant of grace. Often he interpreted the Law in light of the Prophets, who placed emphasis on God's love, mercy and compassionate justice. Jesus did not deal with the Torah as a set of individual rules, each of equal importance. Rather, he laid hold of the essence of the teachings of the Law, which he summarized in quotations from two books of the Law—Deuteronomy 6:5 and Leviticus 19:8. These texts describe God's relationship with persons in terms of love, and the relationships of persons to each other in terms of love, as is appropriate to a covenant of grace. He said, "On these two commandments [to love] hang *all the law and the prophets*." (See Mt. 22:34-40, italics added.) In his view, love of God and of other persons are the appropriate human responses to God's loving acts within the covenant of grace. What Jesus taught about the Law and the Prophets he demonstrated in his actions toward persons. He said doing deeds of mercy on the Sabbath fulfilled the laws governing the Sabbath. For this reason, he did not hesitate to heal persons on the Sabbath. See Lu. 6:6-11.) In his view, the forgiveness of the sins of an adulteress rather than her death by stoning, as literally commanded in the Torah, fulfilled the law. (See Jn. 8:3-11). He used the phrase, "You have heard that it was said," as a way of referring to a legalistic application of the teachings of the Torah. He followed this statement with, "But I say unto you . . .," as a way of showing the Law's fulfillment in the covenant of grace. (See Mt. 5:21-48.)

In many instances, what Jesus taught was a radical alternative to a legalistic application of the Torah. Referring to the laws that provided for various forms of retaliation for injuries suffered (i.e. Ex. 21:23-24; Lev. 24:19-20), Jesus said, "Do not resist an evildoer. But if anyone strikes you on the right cheek, turn the other also" (Mt. 5:39). In other instances Jesus went beyond a legalistic application of the Torah, and emphasized the attitude or motive that lay behind the observance of its laws. A case in point was the law against adultery. "But I say to you that everyone who looks at a woman with lust has already committed adultery with her in his heart" (Mt. 5:28).

The approach of Jesus to the interpretation and application of the Torah (Law) is clearly incompatible with a definition of the divine-human relationship in terms of a covenant of law. Nothing less than a covenant of grace will accommodate such generosity of spirit, such willingness to forgive, such self-giving love. It was that act of supreme self-giving love on the Cross, and the victory over sin and death in the Resurrection that finally illuminated the meaning of the birth of Jesus and the thrust of his teachings and actions. Only in the Good News of the death and resurrection of Jesus the Messiah does one encounter the climactic expression of the unqualified foolishness of God's covenant of grace.

In the Death of Christ

In a two covenant theology, the primary covenant of God with persons is the covenant of law. That covenant defines the nature of sin as transgression of the law. Accordingly, a two-covenant theology interprets the death of Christ as a legal satisfaction of the penalty of death imposed by the covenant of law. Both the Westminster Confession and the 1814 Cumberland Presbyterian Confession stated, "The Lord Jesus by his perfect obedience and sacrifice of himself, . . . *hath fully satisfied the justice of his Father*" (WC 6.5; 1814 CPC 8.5, italics added). Satisfaction of the justice of the Father means satisfaction of the terms of the covenant of law.

This interpretation of the death of Jesus as a legal satisfaction of the demands of the law belongs in a theology in which a covenant of law is primary, in which persons understand their relationship to God in a legal rather than a personal sense. Such a theology defines salvation as God's act of legal acquittal of persons under the penalty of death by accepting the death of Jesus the Christ as a substitute. This is a legalistic substitutionary theory of atonement.

A theology based wholly on a covenant of grace understands the meaning of the death of Christ in terms of grace rather than law. The first clue that the 1984 Confession deals with the death of Christ within the covenant of grace is the statement in the Introduction which identifies John 3:16 as the heart of the Confession. This text, which stands at the very beginning of the text of the Confession, sets the drama of salvation in the context of a family rather than a courtroom. This personal, family context allows a description of the death of Jesus the Christ in terms of grace, as an act of the self-giving love of God.

The Confession describes what God did and does in Jesus the Christ as "a mighty act of reconciling love" (3.07). What God has done and does in the death of Jesus the Christ is not to exact a penalty required by law, but to seek reconciliation with sinful persons through suffering, sacrificial love. This is so because the covenant which binds God to the human family is a covenant of grace rather than law. Accordingly, the key word in the Confession is reconciliation, not satisfaction. Salvation is the restoration of a personal relationship, not the fulfillment of the requirements of the law (See COF 3.01, 3.02, 3.07, 3.08, 3.11). In the words of the apostle Paul, "God was in Christ reconciling the world to himself, *not counting their trespasses against them. . . .*" (2 Cor. 5:19, RSV; italics added).

The Confession of Faith says, "God acts to heal the brokenness and alienation caused by sin and to restore the human family to community through the reconciliation effected in Jesus Christ" (3.01). This healing occurs in two ways through the death of Christ. First, God entered personally into sinful human existence by incarnation in Jesus of Nazareth. Second, having freely taken on the humiliation of sinful human existence, God in Christ endured suffering and death because of sin. As Paul noted, in the view of the world, these actions of God are signs of weakness and make the death of God in Christ appear to be utter foolishness. (See 1 Cor. 1:18-31).

The claim that God entered personally into sinful human existence seems to fly in the face of all claims in the Law and the Prophets about the holiness of God. From God's encounter with Moses in the burning bush to the Holiness Code in Leviticus 17-26, the holiness of God strikes awe, if not terror, in the experiences of sinful people. In his vision in the Temple, Isaiah heard one of the seraphs calling out, "Holy, holy, holy is the lord of hosts." The impact of Isaiah's encounter with the holiness of God caused Isaiah to cry out, "Woe is me! I am lost, for I am a man of unclean lips." (See Isa. 6:2 5). Of his encounter in a vision with the holiness of God, Ezekiel said, "When I saw it, I fell on my face . . . " (Ez. 1:28).

Paul was certainly familiar with the emphasis on the holiness of God in the Law and the Prophets, yet he made the astounding claim that God in Christ became sin for the human family, that persons might become righteous. (See 2 Cor. 5:21.) In his letter to the Philippians, Paul said that God in Christ discarded all those characteristics commonly associated with divinity in order to be "born in human likeness. And being found in human form, he humbled himself and became obedient to the point of death—even death on a cross." (See Phil. 2:5-11.)

The 53rd chapter of Isaiah foreshadowed Paul's clear grasp of how God in Jesus the Christ entered personally into sinful human existence. Speaking of the anticipated Messiah, the prophet said that he was "acquainted with infirmity," and "has borne our infirmities." He "was numbered with the transgressors" and "bore the sins of many." (See Isa. 53:3, 4, 12.) The writer of Hebrews puts it this way "He [Jesus Christ] had to become like his brothers and sisters *in every respect*, so that he might become a merciful and faithful high priest in the service of God" (2:17, italics added). Moreover, "He learned obedience through what he suffered" (5:8).

Affirming at the same time that God is perfect in holiness and that God became sin for us appears contradictory. To say that Jesus the Christ became like us in every respect, yet was without sin also appears inconsistent. In similar paradoxical terms, Paul described the Good News of these contradictions as God's foolishness (1 Cor. 1:25).

What Jesus first spoke to the twelve disciples about his impending death, certainly must have seemed to them to be foolishness. (See Mk. 8:31-33.) They could draw no other conclusion than that for the Messiah to be killed would be a sign of weakness. They had heard Jesus say, "Do not resist an evil doer," but they had not comprehended the radical nature of this teaching, nor had they expected him to practice what he preached. They failed to understand that, given the bondage of the human family to sin and death, God's reconciling, self-giving love in Jesus Christ led necessarily to the cross.

God's personal entrance into the realm of sinful human existence in Christ meant that Jesus the Christ, as an act of self-giving love, would die the death of sin. Marvelling at this mystery, Paul said, "Indeed, rarely will anyone die for a righteous person. . . . But God proves his love for us in that while we were sinners Christ died for us" (Rom 5:28). What happened on the Cross was simply that a man named Jesus was put to death, but this human event had universal theological significance. Because God was incarnate in this man, "The death he died, he died to sin, once for all" (Rom. 6:10).

This death of Jesus Christ on the cross was at the same time a manifestation of the suffering, self-giving love of God for persons created in the divine image and a profound judgment on the whole human family for its rebellion against God. Self-giving love which leads to death is magnificent in its humility, but it is not immediately the source of hope. On the contrary, it appears that the forces of evil have triumphed.

The followers of Jesus did not immediately celebrate the death of Jesus as a victory. They did not celebrate on Calvary's hill, singing, "In the Cross of Christ I Glory." Rather, they experienced a day of darkness and mourning. Matthew reports that the whole creation groaned in agony at the apparent victory of death over life. "Darkness came over the whole land . . . The earth shook, and the rocks were split." Against the stark hopelessness of this event rang out the agonizing cry of Jesus of Nazareth, "My God, my God, why have *you* forsaken me?" (Mt. 27:45, 46, 51; italics added).

Confused, disillusioned and frightened, many of the followers of Jesus, including the Twelve, fled the scene of weakness and death. For them the death of Jesus, whom they had proclaimed the Messiah, was the end of all hope. Whatever they may have thought about the courage of Jesus, it seemed to them a foolish, incredible action, surrendering without a fight. Rather than being a source of their salvation, the cross plunged them into darkness and despair. The plaintive comment of the two followers on the road to Emmaus revealed the depth of their misunderstanding, disillusionment and hopelessness. "But we had hoped that he was the one to redeem Israel" (Lu. 24:21).

In the Resurrection of Christ

The apostle Peter gave the first public witness to what great things God had done in Jesus the Messiah. Addressing the people who had gathered on the Day of Pentecost, Peter first recounted the "deeds of power, wonders, and signs that God had done through (Jesus)" (Acts 2:22). Despite all of these things, or perhaps because of them, Jesus had been "crucified and killed by the hands of those outside the law" (Acts 2:23). For Peter, what finally made sense out of this tragic, lawless death of a man who had gone about doing good was the Resurrection. "God raised him up, having freed him from death, because it was impossible for him to be held in its power" (Acts 2:24).

Peter went on to anchor his testimony to the Resurrection in a quotation from a Psalm attributed to David, saying that in this Psalm David had foreseen "the resurrection of the Messiah." (See Ps. 16:8-11.) The point Peter was making was that those on whom the Holy Spirit had fallen were followers of a living, not a dead Messiah. The Good News was not that Jesus the Messiah had been "killed by the hands of those outside the law," but that God had "freed him from death." Confidently and triumphantly Peter said, "Therefore let the *entire house of Israel* know with certainty that God has made him both *Lord and Messiah,* this Jesus whom you crucified" (Acts 2:36, italics added).

To the Jews of the dispersion and proselytes who had gathered to hear Peter speak, the Good News was that the Messiah had finally and truly come. Though Jesus the Messiah had died, God had raised him from death, and he was living and ruling in the world. Peter then called on the people to repent of their sins and unbelief and to acknowledge that this man whom God had raised was both Lord and Messiah (Savior).

The Acts account says that when the people heard the testimony of Peter, "They were cut to the heart" (2:37). For centuries the Jews had looked, longed, and hoped for the coming of the Messiah. Now these people heard that the Messiah had come, and that a group of Jews had rejected him and had conspired with the Roman government to have him crucified. The devastating impact of Peter's charge on his listeners was understandable. They were overcome with a sense of shame and guilt because of the unbelief in and hostility toward the Messiah by their fellow Jews.

Their response was to cry out to Peter and the other apostles, "Brothers, what should *we* do?" (Acts 2:37, italics added) Sensing in them the beginnings of repentance and faith, Peter instructed them immediately, "Repent, and be baptized everyone one of you in the name of Jesus Christ [Messiah] so that your sins may be forgiven; and you will receive the gift of the Holy Spirit" (Acts 2:38). This ritual was exactly what had been required by John the Baptist as evidence that people wanted to be part of the Kingdom of God, except that now believers were to receive baptism in the name of Jesus the Messiah. The Messiah had come in Jesus of Nazareth, had been killed, but had been "freed from death by God," and was living and ruling in the world.

As Peter and the other apostles reflected on the meaning of the whole

Christ event, the Holy Spirit began to do as Jesus had promised, to "teach (them) everything, and remind (them) of all that (he) had said to them" (Jn. 14:26). In particular, they began to understand the meaning of the Cross and to see it in relationship to the Resurrection.

When a group of people gathered at the Temple to hear Peter speak, he interpreted the death of Jesus the Messiah in this manner: "In this way God fulfilled what he had foretold through all the prophets, that his Messiah would suffer" (Acts 3:18). Peter now understood that the Messiah would be the Suffering Servant of Isaiah 53, not a king with political and military power. He would rule in a manner radically different from the rulers of this world. The Cross belonged to the role of the Suffering Servant Messiah.

At the same time, Peter was getting a better grasp of the meaning of the Resurrection, and was showing clearly and forcefully that the resurrection of Jesus the Christ was the heart of the Good News. To those gathered to hear him at the Temple, he said, "You rejected the Holy and Righteous One and . . . killed the Author of Life, whom God raised from the dead" (Acts 3:14). As the resurrected one, Jesus the Messiah was the Author of Life. Finally, Peter set the whole Christ event in the context of what God had promised in the covenant of grace to Abraham and Sarah, and had confirmed through the prophet Moses. Through the birth, life, death and resurrection of Jesus the Messiah, God would bless all the nations of the earth. (See Acts 3:17-26.)

It was the apostle Paul who took this story about the death and resurrection of Jesus the Messiah and shaped into a universal gospel what at first seemed to have been a message only to the lost house of Israel. This was his key role as the witness to the Gentiles. He fulfilled it while remaining faithful to the Law (Torah) and the Prophets, as he understood them in light of God's revelation in Jesus the Messiah.

Paul knew only too well what Peter had said, that the death of Jesus the Messiah was the consequence of the unbelief and hostility of a group of Jews. At one time he had been among those unbelievers. At the same time, he understood that this historical event that had occurred at a particular time in a particular place was a microcosm of the alienation, hostility and sinfulness of the whole human family. In the Roman letter, in a reference to Adam, Paul involved the whole human family in the problem of sin, and the death which is the consequences of sin. (See Rom. 5:6- 14.) That cross which stood on a barren hill outside the city of Jerusalem was at the same time a witness to God's self-giving love in Jesus Christ and a judgment on the sinfulness of the whole human family. It was, however, the judgment of love not the judgment of law.

In a similar manner, Paul took what was first a message of good news to the Jews, and shaped it into a message of hope to all who are in bondage to sin and death. As on the Day of Pentecost, when people of any time and place are cut to the heart and begin to feel guilt and shame because of the Cross, the Holy Spirit is creating repentance and faith in them. It is then that such people will hear gladly that God resurrected the Author of Life, and through him they may receive the gift of eternal life. Thus Paul wrote, "For if we have been united with (Christ) in a death like his (i.e., the death of sin), we will certainly be united with him in a resurrection like his" (Rom 6:5). Throughout his letters Paul emphasized the resurrection of Jesus as the heart of the Good News. His statement in 1 Corinthians 15:17 is typical: "If Christ has not been raised, your faith is futile and you are still in your sins." For Paul, being in one's sins meant being in bondage to death. Thus he wrote, "For as all die in Adam, so all will be made alive in Christ" (1 Cor. 15:22).

This same view of the role of the Resurrection in God's salvation through Jesus Christ appears elsewhere in the general and pastoral epistles. 1 Timothy 1:10 speaks of the grace of God that "has now been revealed through the appearing of our Savior Christ Jesus, who abolished death and brought life and immortality through the gospel." 1 Peter 1:3 claims that God "has given us a new birth into a living hope through the *resurrection of Jesus Christ from the dead.*" (Italics added). Finally, Hebrews 3:14-15 says that Jesus the Messiah destroyed the power of death that he might "free those who all their lives were held in slavery by the fear of death."

The Confession of Faith affirms that God manifested the covenant of grace in the whole Christ event. "Persons are reconciled to (God) by the *life, death and resurrection of Jesus Christ*. (4.12, italics added). Focusing more particularly on the death and resurrection of Jesus the Messiah as twin components of God's mighty act of reconciling love, the Confession says: "Jesus Christ willingly suffered sin and death for every person. On the third day after being crucified, Christ was raised from the dead" (3.09). Finally, the Confession affirms that "God's work of reconciliation in Jesus Christ . . . is communicated [to persons] by the Holy Spirit" (3.11).

For Discussion

1. Looking over your own experience in the church, which portions of the life, death, and resurrection of Jesus Christ appear to receive the most attention in worship? How do you account for the emphasis you see?
2. Reflect on this claim: From the same Scripture (Torah and Prophets), Jesus taught that God deals with persons in accordance with a covenant of grace; while the scribes and Pharisees taught that God deals with persons in accordance with a covenant of law.
3. Have you generally understood the significance of the death of Christ as a satisfaction of the demands of the law? What happens to this view in a theology based on a covenant of grace?
4. In what ways does the judgment of love differ from the judgment of law?
5. What are your reactions to the claim that the resurrection of Jesus the Christ is at the heart of the Gospel? What evidence do you see in the life and work of the church that indicates the church's reactions to this claim?

CHAPTER 6

THE CALL OF THE HOLY SPIRIT

Read Confession of Faith 4.01-4.04 and Scriptures listed for these sections.

Introduction

The call and work of the Holy Spirit relate specifically to God's saving actions in and through Jesus Christ. The call and work of the Holy Spirit are not, however, restricted to God's redemptive work in the world. As the third person of the Trinity, the Holy Spirit is God the Holy Spirit. Wherever and whenever God is saying and doing things in the world, the Holy Spirit is active. For example, Genesis affirms that in the work of creation, "the Spirit of God was moving over the face of the waters" (Gen. 1:2, RSV).

No claim in Scripture is more important in understanding God's covenant of grace with the human family than that God the Holy Spirit calls persons. The Confession claims that God speaks to the human family. Often when God speaks to persons God speaks in the form of a call. The Confession describes the nature and purpose of the kind of speaking God does as the call of God the Holy Spirit.

God's Initiative in Calling

The Confession says that the "one living God who is Father, Son, and Holy Spirit" is a God who speaks (1.02). One mode of that speaking is calling persons. This mode of speaking emphasizes that God takes the initiative in dealing with persons. The Confession describes this initiative when it says, "The call [of the Holy Spirit] precedes all desire, purpose, and intention of the sinner to come to Christ" (4.03). Later, the Confession speaks of "God's initiative to restore relationships" (4.07).

The picture Genesis 3:1-3 draws of the relationship between God and the creatures made in the divine image is one in which God takes the initiative in seeking personal fellowship with Adam and Eve. While "walking in the garden at the time of the evening breeze," God called out to them, "Where are you?" This call signified God's initiative, and reflected personal concern about the divine-human relationship. This personal concern is God's grace. From that point on, throughout the Old

Testament, God takes the initiative in calling persons, manifesting a concern for their welfare.

It was at this divine initiative that God called Abraham and Sarah, and bound them and their descendants with a covenant promise: "I will make a covenant between me and you, and will make you exceedingly numerous" (Gen. 17:2). Here the call was not simply with the present—"Where are you?" It was also about the future; about who they would become by the grace of God. This covenant of grace in which God called Abraham and Sarah is an act of divine election.

Evidence in the Old Testament of God's faithfulness to the covenant of grace appears in subsequent stories about the divine initiative in calling persons. God heard the groaning of the Israelites in Egypt, and remembered his covenant with Abraham, Isaac, and Jacob. In faithfulness to that covenant, "God called to [Moses] out of the bush," saying, "I have come down to deliver [the Israelites] from the Egyptians." (See Ex. 2:23–3:12.) Accounts of the mighty acts of God's salvation in the exodus became the context in which subsequent Old Testament writers affirmed the divine call and election of Israel.

The prophets became the primary witnesses to God's gracious call and election of Israel. When Israel rebelled against the divine call, God continued to call them through the prophets. Through Hosea, God said, "When Israel was a child, I loved him, and out of Egypt I called my son" (Hos. 11:1). Later, in reference to the forthcoming deliverance of Israel from Babylonian captivity, the prophets emphasize the personal nature of God's call. Through the prophet, God said, "Do not fear, for I have redeemed you; I have *called you by name*, you are mine" (Isa. 43:1, italics added).

The Confession says, "The call . . . of the Holy Spirit is solely of God's grace" (4.03). The fact that God takes the initiative in calling persons is a sign of divine grace. Though demonstrated repeatedly throughout the Old Testament, God's covenant of grace was only partially revealed through the persons and events of that story. It was in God's incarnation in Jesus the Messiah that the fullness of the covenant of grace found expression. Speaking of the Incarnation, the Gospel of John says, "From his (Christ's) fullness we have all received grace upon grace" (Jn. 1:17).

The writer of Hebrews said that God no longer calls to the human family "in many and various ways through the prophets, but in these last days he has spoken to us by a Son . . . (who) is the reflection of God's glory and the exact imprint of God's very being" (1:1). God's calling through the Son had such power and directness the Gospel of Mark records of people who heard Jesus that "They were astonished at his teachings, for he taught them as one having authority, not as the scribes" (Mk. 1:22).

Throughout his ministry, both in word and deed, Jesus the Messiah called people into a community based on the covenant of grace. Through his teachings and finally through his act of self-giving love on the cross, Jesus showed his followers what it meant to be the called of God, God's elect. It is not surprising then, that the second generation of his followers still referred to themselves as the called of God. The author of Hebrews reminds his readers that they are holy partners in a heavenly calling (Heb. 3:1). 2 Timothy urges Christians to remember that God "called [them] with a holy calling" (1:9).

Universality of God's Calling

The Confession says that God acts "with the same intent in the Holy Spirit to *call every person* to repentance and faith" (4.01, italics added). This is so because of the universal problem of sin. The Confession confirms this claim in 2.04: "As did Adam and Eve, all persons rebel against God and lose the right relationship to God, and become slaves to sin and death." Because of the universality of sin, as God called out to Adam and Eve, so God calls out to all people, "Where are you?"

In calling people back into a right relationship, God created a family bound by a covenant of grace. The first clear witness to this covenant of grace which binds God to the human family is in the story of Abraham and Sarah. (See Gen. 12:1-3; 17:1-8.) Abraham and Sarah were Hebrew people. For a time the covenant community consisted of blood descendants of Abraham and Sarah. There is ample evidence, however, that it was never God's intention that the covenant community be restricted to the Hebrew people. God said to Abraham and Sarah, "In you shall all the families of the earth be blessed" (Gen. 12:3).

Though often overlooked, evidence appears early in the Old Testament that God was calling other peoples besides Hebrews. As promised in the covenant with Abraham and Sarah, through their descendants God was calling other people. Moses married a Midianite, and through this relationship, God called the Midianites into the covenant community. (See Ex. 2:15- 22; 18:1-23; Num. 10:29-38.) In fact, one account of the exodus says that "a mixed crowd went up" with the Israelites as they were leaving Egypt (Ex. 12:30). The scripture provides no explanation of who comprised this mixed crowd, but it appears that they shared with the Israelites in the Sinai experience and went with them into the land of Canaan. It is probable that they were other Semitic peoples, like the

Midianites, who intermarried with the Hebrew people. This may explain provisions in the Torah for the integration of foreigners into the covenant community. (See Lev. 19:33-34; Num. 9:14.)

It was the prophets, however, who were most vocal in their protest against Hebrew ethnic exclusiveness in the covenant community, and who were most explicit in reporting God's call of other people. Through the prophet Amos, God said bluntly, "Are you not like the Ethiopians to me, O people of Israel? . . . Did I not bring Israel up from Egypt and the Philistines from Caphtor and the Arameans from Kir?" (9:7). Indeed, God sent Jonah to call the Assyrians of Nineveh into the covenant community, and by the grace of God the Assyrians responded to the call in repentance and faith, despite the outright hostility of the Hebrew messenger. It is not surprising that in a vision of the messianic age found in Isaiah, God said, "Blessed be Egypt my people, and Assyria the work of my hands, and Israel my heritage" (19:25). Finally, the prophet Joel gave the most direct witness to the universality of the call of God's Holy Spirit. In a vision of the messianic age, he reported these words of God: "I will pour out my spirit on *all flesh*" (2:18, italics added).

The New Testament quickly reaffirms the testimony of the Old Testament to God's gracious call to the whole human family. The song of the angels at the birth of Jesus the Messiah was, "good news of great joy for *all people*" (Lu. 2:10, italics added). God's messenger, John the Baptist, called out to all who would listen, "Repent, for the kingdom of heaven has come near" (Mt. 3:2). He explicitly rejected any exclusive ethnic Hebrew claim on citizenship in the messianic kingdom, saying that God could raise up children to Abraham from stones (Mt. 3:9).

Throughout his ministry, Jesus called people, without distinction, to repent of their sins and to acknowledge the rule of God in their lives. His ministry to Samaritans and to the people of Tyre and Sidon, and the commission he gave to his disciples indicated his determination to extend his rule as Messiah beyond ethnic Hebrew limits. (See Mt. 28:19-20; Mk. 7:14 37; Jn. 4:7-30.)

On the Day of Pentecost, Peter cited the passage from Joel 2:28 and claimed that the events that were occurring were signs within the present reality of the messianic age, where the risen Messiah ruled as Lord and Savior. Through the people on whom the Holy Spirit fell that day, God began to call others, Jews and Gentiles, throughout the whole Mediterranean world. A dramatic break in the ethnic Hebrew exclusiveness came in the witness of Peter to Cornelius and his household and friends, and in the subsequent meeting of the followers of Jesus in Jerusalem. James, who presided at the Jerusalem meeting, said, "My brothers, listen to me.

Simon (Peter) has related how God first looked favorably on Gentiles, to take from them a people for his name." (See Acts 10:9-48; 15:6-21.) The apostle Paul, who himself experienced the call of God as he travelled from Jerusalem to Damascus, became one of the foremost witnesses to and interpreters of the call of God to Gentiles. In his letter to the Galatians, he argued that Gentiles were included in God's call to Abraham, Sarah and their descendants. (See Gal. 3:6-9.) Later, in his letter to the Romans, Paul gave witness to the mercy of God for "including us whom he (God) has called, not from the Jews only but also from the Gentiles" (Rom. 9:24).

God's Ways of Calling

The Confession says that "God's work of reconciliation in Jesus Christ . . . is communicated by the Holy Spirit, and through such instruments as God is pleased to employ" (3.11). The Confession goes on to identify some of these instruments. "The Holy Spirit works through the scriptures, the sacraments, the corporate worship of the covenant community, the witness of believers in word and deed, and *in ways beyond human understanding*" (4.02, italics added).

The Scriptures themselves give ample testimony that they have been and are a primary means through which the Holy Spirit calls people. The account in Luke 24:13-27 of the walk to Emmaus by the risen Christ and two of his disciples, says that Jesus the Messiah, beginning with Moses and the prophets, interpreted to those with him things about himself in all the scriptures." Later, before his ascension into heaven, Jesus the Messiah gave "instructions through the Holy Spirit to the apostles whom he had chosen" (Acts 1:2). In light of his conversation with the two disciples on the road to Emmaus, it is reasonable to conclude that the "instructions through the Holy Spirit," which Jesus gave to the apostles, were also from the Law and the Prophets.

The entire book of Acts is about how the Holy Spirit called people through the witness of the followers of Jesus as they interpreted the Law and the Prophets to their listeners. On the Day of Pentecost Peter spoke from a text found in the prophet Joel. Later, in interpreting the meaning of the death of Jesus the Messiah, Peter said, "In this way God fulfilled what he had foretold through all the prophets, that his Messiah would suffer" (Acts 3:18).

The testimony of Stephen in Acts 7 is a summary of the mighty acts of God recounted in the Law and the Prophets. When his listeners rejected this testimony, Stephen said, "You are forever opposing the Holy Spirit, just as your ancestors used to do." (See Acts 7:2-53.) Accounts of Paul's ministry show that when he visited a synagogue, after reading from the Law and the Prophets, he proceeded to interpret the Scriptures in light of the claims that Jesus of Nazareth was the Messiah.

Whether through a sermon, through group study under the direction of a teacher, or study by an individual, God is forever calling people through Scripture. Indeed, the fact that God the Holy Spirit speaks through the Scriptures establishes their validity. As the Confession says, "The authority of the scriptures is founded on the truth contained in them *and the voice of God speaking through them*" (1.06, italics added). The Confession goes on to say that the "illumination of God's own Spirit" is critical to any understanding of what God is saying through the Scriptures (1.07).

It is significant that the Scriptures appear first in the Confession's list of instruments through which the Holy Spirit calls persons. It is relatively easy for individuals to claim that the Holy Spirit has spoken to them, but very difficult for others to test the validity of such claims. One way of evaluating such claims is by reference, not to single verses of Scripture, but to general teachings of the Scriptures.

The Confession lists the sacraments second among the instruments through which the Holy Spirit calls persons. In this respect, baptism is particularly significant. First, baptism is itself a sign of the gift of the Holy Spirit, or of birth by the Holy Spirit. Second, when an infant, at least one of whose parents is a believer, receives baptism, the parents and the congregation covenant with God to teach the child the meaning of his or her baptism. When communities do this teaching faithfully, beginning at the earliest levels of the child's understanding, baptism can be a powerful instrument through which the Holy Spirit will call the child to repentance and faith. The Sacrament of the Lord's Supper, or Holy Communion is another way in which God the Holy Spirit calls believers to greater awareness of God's presence.

Following the sacraments, the Confession lists the corporate worship of the church as an instrument through which the Holy Spirit calls persons to repentance and faith. This claim has been institutionalized in the worship of many Cumberland Presbyterian churches through the invitation that characteristically follows the sermon. This location of the invitation in the order of worship may have intentionally or unintentionally linked the call of the Holy Spirit to the sermon and the invitation hymn. In fact, however, all the components of corporate worship may be instruments of the Holy Spirit, and the worship experience may become the instrument by which the Spirit calls persons days or even months and years later.

The church has historically associated the gift of the Holy Spirit with baptism. The New Testament describes the life of a Christian as a life in the Spirit. Accordingly, the Confession lists "the witness of believers in word and deed" as an instrument through which the Holy Spirit calls other persons. In word and deed, every Christian should consider him/herself an evangelist. If, through the ministry of a congregation, few people seem to be hearing and responding to the call of the Holy Spirit, the situation may be due in large part to the failure of the members, in word and deed, to be effective instruments of that call.

Finally, the Confession says that the Holy Spirit calls persons "in ways that are beyond human understanding" (4.02). In another place, dealing with the witness of the church, the Confession says, "where and when this witness is lacking, God is not without a witness" (5.31). The Confession urges Christians to be sensitive to the mystery of God the Holy Spirit in the world. In particular, Christians should resist the tendency to look no further than ordinary means as the instruments of the Holy Spirit. Before Peter ever arrived in Caesarea, God the Holy Spirit had been calling Cornelius, through means never identified. Cornelius had already begun to respond to the call of God. Through Peter the Holy Spirit put the finishing touches on the call. Every person who seeks to be a witness to the Gospel should remember that before she or he ever speaks to a person, the Holy Spirit has already been calling the person in ways beyond human understanding.

God's Reason for Calling

The Confession says that "the Spirit moves on the hearts of sinners, convincing them of their sins and their need for salvation" (4.02) and goes on to say that this moving or calling by the Holy Spirit "precedes all desire, purpose, and intention of the sinner to come to Christ" (4.03). Taken together, these statements constitute a devastating indictment of humanity, made in the image of God, created to live in a covenant of grace with God. The Confession asserts that they are living in contradiction to their God-given natures.

The reason for this indictment is this: "As did Adam and Eve, all persons rebel against God, lose the right relationship with God, and become slaves to sin and death" (COF 2.04). Unless one takes this radical human predicament seriously, all talk about the call of God the Holy Spirit is pointless. Persons must be convinced that they are sinners, slaves to sin and death, and in need of salvation. This is the reason God asked Adam and Eve, and all their descendants, the probing question: "Where are you?"

The reason for this probing question, the call of God the Holy Spirit, is to confront all persons with their nakedness before God. They must stand naked before God, so that their true condition, their shame may be revealed to them. Their situation is not simply that they have broken some rule or law. Rather, they have wilfully violated the most sacred of all personal relationships, the covenant of grace. They have denied their utter dependence on God for life, and have presumed to be gods themselves. In such circumstances they have neither desire nor ability to come to God. As the Confession says, "They (are) inclined toward sin in all aspects of their being" (2.03).

Sinful persons have in themselves no desire to come to God, for the very nature of their sin is rebellion against God. The essence of this rebellion is the assumption that they can live without God. The apostle Paul described this state of rebellion in this way: "Though they (all persons) knew God, they did not honor him as God or give thanks to him" (Rom. 1:21). They clothe themselves with elaborate deceptions, and exhibit pathetic bravado. As Paul said, "They know God's decree, that those who practice such things (i.e., evils that flow from their rebellion) deserve to die—yet they not only do them but applaud others who practice them" (Rom. 1:32).

God faces a situation in which persons created in the divine image have neither desire, purpose, nor intention to honor God nor to give thanks to God. The situation calls for what the Confession describes as the "illuminating influence of the Holy Spirit." The call of the Holy Spirit seeks to penetrate human rebellion and self-deception, and to lay bare the true human predicament. This is the initial and necessary stage of God's work of redemption.

The human predicament is what Scripture calls "being dead in sin," without hope in the world. (See Eph. 2:1-2; Col. 2:13.) A most graphic picture of this human condition is found in the thirty seventh chapter of Ezekiel, the vision of the valley of dry bones. In this graveyard, the dead people say, "Our bones are dried up, and our hope is lost; we are cut off completely" (Ez. 37:11). Whether or not these dead persons will live again is entirely at God's discretion. Simply put, people who are in bondage to sin and death can't make the first move. It is this condition which the illuminating influence of the Holy Spirit seeks to set out in bold relief, and thereby induce persons to cry out for help.

People's Response to God's Calling

As unbelievable as it may seem,"persons may resist and reject the call of the Holy Spirit" (COF 4.04). The combination of a rebellious spirit and suppressed feelings of guilt causes persons to turn a deaf ear to the call of the Holy Spirit. In all creation only human creatures, made in the image of God, have exhibited such arrogance. This is the ultimate consequence of believing the deceptive claim that persons may become gods themselves, capable of freely determining their own destinies.

The understanding of the bondage of alcoholism developed by Alcoholics Anonymous provides a close parallel to the theological understanding of bondage to sin and death. In both cases resistance to the very suggestion that one is not in control occurs. In the case of an alcoholic, a loving spouse may take the risk of personal destruction by refusing to forsake the one in bondage. God in Jesus Christ took that very risk by refusing to forsake the human family in bondage to sin and death. It was this self-giving love that led God in Christ to death on a cross.

The Good News is that, in spite of persons' resistance to and rejection of the call of the Holy Spirit, God never forsakes the creatures made in the divine image. People of the church at Ephesus received a description of the persistence of the call of the Holy Spirit, and the miracle of God's redeeming grace: "God who is rich in mercy, and out of the great love with which he loved us even when we were dead through our trespasses, made us alive together with Christ—by grace you have been saved . . ." (Eph. 2:4-5).

When Christians reflect honestly and thankfully on the miracle of God's saving grace in Jesus the Christ, mediated through the Holy Spirit, they give joyful testimony to God's election. The doctrine of election is not a theory about why God chose some people and not others before the foundation of the world or at any other time. Rather, in the words of that hymn which celebrates the amazing grace of God, talk about God's election is the witness of a redeemed sinner: "I once was lost, but now I am found, was blind but now I see."

John Newton, the author of "Amazing Grace," was a slave trader. He had witnessed the utter hopelessness of men and women, bound in the hold of a slave ship, destined to a life of slavery. Through this experience etched in his memory and burned into his conscience, the Holy Spirit led John Newton to understand that in the most profound sense of his personal condition and destiny, this was his predicament. He knew that he was hopelessly lost, bound in the hold of sin's slave ship, on the way to eternal hell. He knew that he had not found Jesus, for he was blind and couldn't see. Rather, God in Christ had found him, given him sight, and set him free.

It is in this sense, and this sense only, that a Christian, and only a Christian, can understand and give witness to God's election, the wonder of God's redeeming grace. Though it is a joyful testimony, it finds its purest expression in humility, for redeemed sinners know that they did not choose God. Rather, God chose them, and in love called and claimed them through the Holy Spirit, inducing in them genuine repentance and bestowing on them the gift of faith. By contrast, all general discussions of the doctrine of election will always founder on the perilous rocks of freedom of will and divine sovereignty.

What is at issue is not freedom to choose Jesus, but freedom to love God. The freedom to love a person against whom you have sinned and from whom you are alienated, comes only through a free, unconditioned act of forgiveness by the one against whom the sin has occurred. So it is with the sinner and God. When confronted by such self-giving love, the sinner may be cut to the heart, and, falling down, cry out in repentance and shame, acknowledging that he or she is unworthy of such love. However, the free, unconditional, and self-giving love of God will not let go. God in Christ reaches out, lifts sinners up, and plants their feet on the solid ground, giving them the faith to entrust themselves to God.

God's election is a miracle of grace. In this election, redeemed persons know that they belong to God's elect, the covenant family of God. What has occurred is nothing less than their resurrection from the dead. In the words of Ephesians 2:4-5, redeemed sinners are able to testify, "God, who is rich in mercy, out of the great love with which he has loved us even when we were dead through our trespasses, made us alive together with Christ."

Any attempt to convert the doctrine of election into anything more than a witness by a redeemed sinner to the miracle of God's grace leads to what 2 Timothy 2:23 calls "stupid and senseless controversies." Unredeemed sinners know why they have not been resurrected from death to life. It is because they have persisted in arrogant rebellion against the God who loves them. Redeemed sinners, awed by the mystery and miracle of their salvation, are constrained to give glory only to God. Yes, they have responded to God's grace in Jesus Christ, but only because the Spirit of God moved on their hearts, "inclining them to repentance and faith toward God." (See COF 4.02.)

Ironically, most discussions of the miracles reported in Scripture have focused on such things as turning water into wine or walking on water, and have ignored the greatest miracle of all—the resurrection to new life of persons who are in bondage to sin and death.

For Discussion

1. What does it mean to say that God's call renders persons naked before God?
2. How do you react to the claim that God's call and election of Abraham and Sarah was never intended by God to be understood as restricted to the ethnic group called the Hebrews?
3. As you reflect on your own call out of bondage to sin and death into the freedom of God's love in the family of God, what were the means through which this call has come? What were the evidences of God's initiative?
4. How do you react to the claim of the Confession that it is God's call that creates the "desire, purpose and intention of the sinner to come to Christ"—that of themselves sinners would never turn to God?
5. How do you react to the claim that only the redeemed sinner can know the meaning of God's call and election—can have any sense of the miracle of God's grace in salvation?

CHAPTER 7

THE WORK OF THE HOLY SPIRIT: SALVATION

Read Confession of Faith 4.05-4.20 and Scriptures listed for these sections.

Introduction

Persons experience salvation from sin, liberation from bondage to sin and death. The experience of salvation is at the same time what God the Holy Spirit does, and what persons do in response to the call of God's Spirit. The experience of salvation cannot be dissected, however, with parts to be credited to God and other parts to persons. Though persons are not passive in their salvation, it is appropriate to describe salvation as wholly the work of God the Holy Spirit. In the hymn "Amazing Grace," John Newton celebrated this work of God. He shared the view of the apostle Paul, who said that salvation "depends not on human will or exertion, but on God who shows mercy" (Rom. 9:16).

God's salvation of persons occurs as a miracle of God's grace. As such, it partakes of the mystery that always characterizes the work of God in the world. Persons saved in Christ through the work of the Holy Spirit can speak meaningfully of the experience. However, what they are able to say is not so much an explanation of what occurred, as it is a hymn of thanksgiving for the grace of God by which they have been set free from bondage to sin and death. In the words of the blind man who was healed by Jesus, when asked for an explanation of what had occurred: "One thing I do know, that though I was blind, now I see" (Jn. 9:25). What follows is not so much an explanation of what happens in the experience of salvation, as a reflection by persons who know that once they were lost but now are saved. Meaningful discussion of salvation is not so much explanation of how salvation occurs as testimony of persons who stand in awe at the grace of God in the life, death and resurrection of Jesus the Christ. It is a testimony in which persons make no claim about what they have done, but who give God all the glory.

The Work of Repentance

The call of the Holy Spirit renders persons naked before God. The illuminating influence of the Holy Spirit puts persons under the spotlight of God, showing them who they are—creatures who have rebelled against their Creator. They have embraced the deception that they are gods, capable of determining their own destinies. The Confession says that this moving by the Holy Spirit on persons is for the purpose of "convincing them of their sins and their need for salvation, and *inclining them to repentance* . . . toward God" (4.02; italics added).

Repentance is not simply what persons do. While it is the case that people repent of their sins, they have within themselves neither the desire nor the ability to repent. Persons who repent must acknowledge they have been inclined to do so by the Holy Spirit (COF 4.02). The Holy Spirit, in a miracle of grace, somehow breaks or alters the inclination of persons to rebel against God and inclines them to repent of this rebellion. Repentance is a human response to what God has done which persons are enabled to do by the Holy Spirit. The Confession puts it this way: "In response to God's initiative to restore relationships, persons make honest confession of sin against God . . .. (4.07).

In its most fundamental sense, repentance is not of the nature of an apology to God for having committed some particular sin. Rather, it is the cry of a desperate person in a hopeless situation. The reason for this desperation is that at one time all persons are "slaves to sin and death" (COF 2.04). The Confession goes on to describe this predicament as "spiritual death" (4.16). The Holy Spirit even places this desperate cry for help itself on the lips of a penitent person. This is the reason that the Confession says, "Persons do not merit salvation because of repentance" (4.06). Persons cannot claim that it was they who finally decided, in a last burst of energy and in an exercise of freedom of will, to cry, "Help!"

This radical view of repentance as the work of the Holy Spirit is matched by an equally radical description of the nature and scope of repentance. It is an "attitude toward God wherein sinners firmly resolve to forsake sin, trust in Christ, and live in grateful obedience to God" COF 4.05). This means that repentance is not a one time event. Genuine repentance is a disposition of the whole person, a humility of spirit renewed daily by the continuing work of the Holy Spirit. It is neither accidental nor surprising that the devotional literature of the great saints reflects a continuing sensitivity to and need for repentance; nor that with Paul, they describe themselves as "chief of all sinners" (See 1 Tim. 1:19).

The scope of repentance for persons is nothing less than the scope of their sin. According to the Confession, the basic sin of persons is not simply against God, but against the rest of creation as well. As a consequence of the sin of persons, "the whole creation stands in need of God's redemption" (COF 2.06). The Holy Spirit calls persons to "make honest confession of sin against God, *their brothers and sisters, and all creation, and amend the past so far as in their power*" (COF 4.07; italics added).

One of the glaring deficiencies in the church's approach to evangelism today is the almost total disregard of the work of the Holy Spirit in repentance. The usual approach is simply to ask persons to accept Jesus Christ as personal Savior, by coming forward in a service of worship and giving the minister a handshake. This relatively painless process of becoming a Christian ignores both the reality of the sinner's state of rebellion against God and the resultant bondage to sin and death. It bypasses the radical experience of repentance as a necessary condition for the gift of faith.

The Protestant reformation abolished the sacrament of penance. However, the fact that the Confession of Faith has a section entitled "Repentance and Confession" means that what was embodied in the sacrament of penance is nevertheless of fundamental importance. That is, the church must give serious attention to some means whereby persons may exhibit the spirit and fruits of repentance. As the Confession insists, genuine repentance is not simply toward God, but toward other persons and toward the natural world.

Alcoholics Anonymous has grasped the essential nature of sin as a bondage from which persons cannot free themselves. This organization has also understood the meaning of genuine repentance. Alcoholics who finally in desperation cry, "Help," are guided into a serious demonstration of repentance. This includes confession to persons they have wronged, payment of debts previously avoided, and performance of deeds of kindness to other persons in need. The church would do well to think through how it might become the instrument of the Holy Spirit in guiding persons through the rigorous experience of making amends for past sins against "God, their brothers and sisters, and all creation, . . . so far as in their power" (COF 4.07).

The Work of Saving Faith

Like repentance, faith is a work of the Holy Spirit. Though faith is a response of persons, it is "prompted by the Holy Spirit" (COF 4.08). In language even more radical than that used to describe repentance, the Confession says plainly that "faith is a gift made possible through God's love and initiative" (4.09). The Scripture describes the miracle of God's grace in saving persons through faith: "God, who is rich in mercy, and out of the great love with which he loved us *even when we were dead in our trespasses,* made us alive together with Christ . . . . For by grace you have been saved through faith, and this is not your own doing; *it is a gift of God*—not the result of works, so that no one may boast" (Eph. 2:4,5,8,9, italics added).

The passage makes clear that, though a human response, faith is a gift of God, "so that no one may boast." The Confession affirms this explanation of the nature of faith in this way: "Persons do not merit salvation because of faith, nor is faith a good work" (4.09). Persons can take no credit for exercising faith. As in the case of repentance, sinners have neither the desire nor the ability to respond to God in faith. Before persons receive the gift of faith, they are dead in their trespasses, in rebellion against God. After they receive the gift of faith, they live new lives.

The Confession defines faith as trust in God. It is "trust in the truthfulness of God's promises in scripture" (4.08). If, as the Introduction to the Confession claims, John 3:16 is "the gospel in miniature," then the essence of "God's promises in scripture" is in God's covenant of grace. Because of that covenant, God the Holy Spirit never ceases working to create in rebellious, alienated persons the desire and ability to entrust themselves to God. As the Confession says, the Holy Spirit both instructs "persons savingly in the knowledge of God" and leads "them to believe God" (3.04).

The Confession states that faith includes "sorrow for sin, and determination to serve God and neighbor" (4.08). Genuine repentance, then, is a precondition of faith. Repentance and faith are the reverse sides of the same work of God the Holy Spirit. This work of the Holy Spirit has at the same time dissolved the inclination of rebellion against and the alienation of persons toward God and created in them an inclination to repent of their sins and trust and love God.

In a similar sense, God the Holy Spirit enables persons both to "amend the past" and gives them a "determination to serve God and neighbor." (See COF 4.07, 4.08.) This miracle of grace both liberates persons from bondage to sin and death and creates them as new persons in Christ Jesus. This is what the Confession means when it says that in faith persons both "receive forgiveness for their sins and experience acceptance as God's children" (4.10). That is, this miracle of God's grace pertains not only to what persons have been, but to what by the grace of God they may become.

When persons experience acceptance as God's children, the focus of concern shifts from the past to the future. Faith is that relationship of trust in God in which believers are tested and suffer many struggles. The Confession calls the Christian life a "life of faith," in which "ultimate victory through Christ is assured by God's faithfulness" (4.11). The victory of faith is not won by the effort of the believer to hold out until the end. Rather, God's faithfulness assures it.

The Work of Justification

The Confession describes faith as a "response to God, prompted by the Holy Spirit, wherein persons rely solely upon God's grace in Christ for salvation" (4.05). Scripture sometimes describes this salvation as justification before God. The term justification may suggest the experience of acquittal of a criminal who stands judged before the law. This is, in fact, the meaning both the 1814 and 1883 Cumberland Presbyterian Confessions give. Both of these confessions understood a covenant of law as the original and continuing primary covenant which bound God to the human family. Given the covenant of law, it is understandable that justification would have been described as "strictly a legal transaction" (1883 COF, Sec. 49).

The 1984 Confession rejects the concept of a covenant of law on the grounds that Scripture, understood in light of the birth, death, and resurrection of Jesus Christ, does not teach such a concept. Understood in the context of the covenant of grace, as set forth in the 1984 Confession, "Justification is God's loving acceptance of believers whereby persons are reconciled to him by the life, death, and resurrection of Jesus Christ" (4.12).

Two key terms exist in the definition of justification. First, justification is God's act of loving acceptance. Both the personal nature of the covenant of grace and the quality of self giving love in the relationship that covenant establishes are important. In another place, the Confession describes God's act of self giving love in this way: "Jesus Christ *willingly suffered sin and death* for every person" (3.09; italics added). Second, justification is God's act of reconciliation with those in whom the Holy Spirit has done the works of repentance and faith. In reconciliation God's act of loving acceptance has overcome their rebellion and alienation.

The life, death, and resurrection of Jesus Christ accomplishes justification, personal acceptance and reconciliation (4.12). The whole Christ event deserves attention as God's saving act. Salvation was not and is not accomplished solely on the Cross, but by the life, death and resurrection of Jesus Christ. A major deficiency of evangelical Protestant worship and witness, including prayers, hymns/songs, sermons and personal testimonies, has been their almost exclusive focus on the Cross as the event in which God accomplished and continues to accomplish salvation.

Emphasis on the saving power of the whole Christ event in no way detracts from the significance of the Cross. When one understands salvation as justification, or personal reconciliation to God, the death of Christ reveals God's reconciling love. John 3:16 fully expresses the meaning of the Cross, God's act of self-giving love. As Paul put it in 1 Corinthians 5:19, "In Christ God was reconciling the world to himself, not counting their trespasses against them." Even more directly, Paul wrote to the Romans, "God proved his love for us in that while we were sinners, Christ died for us" (Rom. 5:8). As God's saving action, the death of Christ suggested to the author of Hebrews a parallel with the sin offering in the worship of ancient Israel. "[Jesus the Christ] entered once for all into the Holy Place, not with the blood of goats and bulls, but with his own blood, thus obtaining eternal redemption" (9:12). An examination of the relevant texts in the Law (Torah) on the sin offering will uncover all the imagery associated with the shedding of blood.

According to the Law, the very essence of life is in the blood; thus the offering of the blood of an animal in worship signified the costly character of reconciliation between God and sinful persons. The author of Hebrews asserts, "Under the law almost everything is purified with blood, and without the shedding of blood there is no forgiveness of sin" (9:22). Reconciliation in relationships between God and persons comes at the cost of life itself, the life of God in Jesus the Christ. According to Hebrews, "The law has only a shadow of the good things to come and not the true form of these realities" (10:1). This means that the real cost of reconciliation between God and persons was not in the sacrifice of animals, but when the blood of God in Christ was shed on Calvary for the sins of the world. How unthinkable! What foolishness! God in Christ "bore our sins in his body on the cross, so that, free from sin, we might live for righteousness" (I Pet. 2:24). In the words of the Confession, "Jesus Christ willingly suffered sin and death for every person" (3.09). It is in the proclamation of this foolishness about God's self-giving love in the death of Christ, that the Holy Spirit moves on the hearts of sinners convincing them of their sins and their need for salvation, and inclining them to repentance and faith toward God.

For Christians, one of the most frustrating and often puzzling aspects of the experience of God's salvation through Jesus Christ is what the Confession calls the continuing presence of a sinful nature. The Confession puts it this way: "They [Christians] continue to experience within themselves the conflict between their old selves and their new selves, between good and evil, between their wills and the will of God" (4.14). Some have called this condition a case of theological schizophrenia. This condition sometimes results in self-denial, an unwillingness to face up to the continuing presence of a sinful nature. 1 John 1:8 recognizes and addresses such self-denial: "If we (Christians) say we have no sin, we deceive ourselves, and the truth is not in us." The letter goes on to explain this theological schizophrenia by distinguishing between the times when persons act like children of the devil and times when they act like children of God. (See 1 Jn. 3:1-10.) Recognizing this disparity between the persons that Christians are called to be and the persons they actually are, the Confession says, "Only by growth in grace can the believer experience the fullness of relationship with God" (4.13).

The other side of the issue of a continuing sinful nature in persons who have been justified by God in an act of loving acceptance is the fear that they might lose their salvation. The Confession speaks to this concern in this way: "In this relationship God continues to forgive sin. Although believers sometimes disrupt their peace with God through sin and experience separation from God, yet they are assured that it is by God's grace that they are accepted and the relationship is sustained" (4.13).

The Work of Regeneration or New Birth and Adoption

The Scriptures use a wealth of terms and metaphors to describe the miracle of God's grace in the salvation of rebellious, alienated sinners. Each term or metaphor reveals a different insight into an event that is indescribably rich in meaning and possibilities. This wealth of language in Scripture makes it possible for persons of radically different backgrounds to communicate something of the richness of their own experiences of the grace of God in Jesus Christ. The terms justification, regeneration, new birth and adoption are examples. They do not refer to different parts of the experience of salvation, but are different ways of talking about a miracle of God's grace that always remains a mystery. The Confession of Faith says, "Those who trust in Jesus Christ are recreated, born again, renewed in spirit and made new persons in Christ" (4.15). The Confession uses two metaphors, regeneration and new birth, as synonyms, but each communicates its own insight into the nature of the experience of salvation. This kind of language is compatible with a description in the Confession of the human predicament, in which persons are said to be "spiritually dead and unable of themselves to love and glorify God" (COF 4.16).

Regeneration explores the meaning of salvation, not as a restoration of broken relationships (justification), but as being resurrected from death to life. The Confession says, "Those who trust in Jesus Christ are recreated, or born again, renewed in spirit and made new persons in Christ" (4.25). This kind of language is compatible with a description of the human predicament, in which persons are described as "spiritually dead and unable of themselves to love and glorify God" (COF 4.16). Using the term regeneration to describe the experience of salvation puts the resurrection of Jesus the Christ at the center of the drama of salvation. If the human predicament is that persons are in bondage to sin and death, then the hope of being delivered from this bondage is in the resurrection of Jesus Christ. Paul says that Jesus Christ "died to sin, once for all," but "being raised from the dead, will never die again; death no longer has dominion over him." It follows, then, that "if we have been united with him in death like his, we will certainly be united with him in a resurrection like his." (See Rom. 6:5-11.)

In the first letter to the Corinthians, Paul related salvation from sin to the resurrection of Christ. He wrote, "If Christ has not been raised, your faith is futile and you are still in your sins" 1 Cor. 15:17). Other writings in the New Testament explicitly associate the new birth with the resurrection of Christ. One example occurs in 1 Peter 1:3: "By (God's) great mercy he has given us a new birth into a living hope *through the resurrection of Jesus Christ from the dead* (italics added).

The concept of a new birth for those who are dead in trespasses and sin comes directly from the teachings of Jesus, from his conversation with Nicodemus. Jesus said to Nicodemus, "Very truly, I tell you, no one can see the kingdom of God without being born from above" (Jn. 3:3). Jesus also described this rebirth as being born of the Spirit. Earlier the Gospel of John speaks of persons who "become children of God, who (are) born, not of blood or the will of the flesh or the will of man, but of God" (1:12-13).

Nicodemus did not easily grasp the radical nature of this theological concept. It was foreign to the thinking of teachers of Judaism in that day. John the Baptist had laid the groundwork for the concept by challenging the commonly held assumption that anyone who was a blood descendant of Abraham and Sarah was assured of citizenship in the Kingdom of God. John laid out the further conditions of repentance and baptism. At the same time, he anticipated the concept of a new birth in the Spirit, when he said that the Messiah would baptize not with water but with the Holy Spirit.

In addition to blood descent from Abraham and Sarah, Nicodemus and other teachers of Judaism of that day had added the condition of faithful obedience of the Law. However, they taught that faithful obedience of the Law could be performed only by an ethnic Hebrew, or a Gentile who had become a proselyte. The concept of an event in which persons, Jews or Gentiles, became new persons was difficult to grasp. Nicodemus asked, "How can these things be?" (Jn. 3:9).

The concept of a new birth was difficult for the teachers of Judaism to grasp, in part, because they had no understanding of original sin. The view that all persons, Jews and Gentiles alike, live in alienation from God and in bondage to sin and death was foreign to their thinking. It is only in the context of such an understanding of the radical predicament of the human family that the doctrine of the new birth makes sense.

The concept of the new birth which Jesus introduced gave insights into both the nature of the salvation of unredeemed sinners and the nature of God who saves. Jesus taught his followers both to pray to God as Father, and to think of God as the one who gave them birth. Fathers share in the conception of children, but it is mothers who give them birth. It is significant that Jesus spoke of being born of God the Holy Spirit, for the New Testament represents the Holy Spirit by a feminine symbol, the dove. (See Mt. 3:16; Mk. 1:10; Lu. 3:22; Jn. 1:32.)

The Confession says not only that persons are "recreated, or born again, renewed in spirit and made new persons in Christ," but also that they are adopted into "the covenant family" (4.20). The analogy of adoption comes from Paul's letter to the Galatians. Paul first used the term in reference to Jews, who through Jesus Christ, were set free from bondage to the law. "God sent his son, born of woman, born under the law, in order to redeem those who were born under the law, so that they might receive adoption as children" (Gal. 4:4-5). In Romans 8:14-15 and in Ephesians the term receives universal application. "[God] destined us [Jews and Gentiles] for adoption as his children through Jesus Christ" (Eph. 1:5).

Paul's use of the concept of adoption reflects his sensitivity to the culture of the Roman world, and his need to use concepts familiar to that culture. No laws for adoption are found in the Old Testament, nor is their much evidence that the practice existed in Jewish communities in New Testament times. By contrast, there were Roman laws of adoption, and the practice was common in the Roman world. Indeed, this concept is particularly meaningful to Christian families in the United States today, where children often become members of families through adoption.

Whether understood as justification, regeneration (new birth) or adoption, the miracle and mystery of God's salvation is and always has been the occasion of wonder and praise by those who are redeemed through Jesus Christ. This miracle and mystery continues in the sanctification and growth in grace of those who have been and are being saved.

For Discussion

1. What is/was your own personal experience of salvation? If you are studying with a group, discuss this with a partner or in a small group. Must everyone be able to point to an event of salvation? Is it possible to speak of salvation as a lifelong process?
2. React to the view that the experience of salvation cannot be dissected, with certain parts credited to persons and other parts to God. How helpful is it to think in terms of thankfulness to God instead of in terms of understanding everything God is doing?
3. Do you agree or disagree with the claim that the evangelistic work of the church today fails to stress the scope of the work of the Holy Spirit in repentance? Discuss your reactions with a group.
4. Is it helpful for you personally to understand justification before God more in terms of personal reconciliation instead of legal acquittal? How does your understanding of human relationships inform your thinking in this area?
5. In what way does the description of the experience of salvation as regeneration or a new birth focus attention on the resurrection of Jesus Christ as the key event in the Good News?

CHAPTER 8

THE WORK OF THE HOLY SPIRIT: CONTINUING SALVATION

Read Confession of Faith 4.21-4.29 and Scriptures listed for these sections.

Introduction

The Confession of Faith describes the experience of salvation under the general heading, "God Acts Through the Holy Spirit." This means that from beginning to end, salvation is the work of God the Holy Spirit. In an objective sense, God accomplishes the work of salvation in the birth, life, death and resurrection of Jesus the Messiah. As persons experience that salvation, it is the work of the Holy Spirit. Both in its objective reality and as it is experienced by persons, salvation is of the grace of God. It occurs and believers experience it because of and within the covenant of grace.

In reflecting on the miracle and mystery of God's grace, and guided by Scripture, persons have described different dimensions of what they have experienced. This reflective description has yielded such terms as the call of the Holy Spirit, repentance, confession, saving faith, justification, regeneration, new birth, and adoption. Under the same general heading, the Confession includes other significant, descriptive terms: sanctification, growth in grace, preservation of believers, and Christian assurance. These works of the Holy Spirit do not come after salvation; they are dimensions of the continuing miracle and mystery of God's saving grace.

Neither a logical nor a necessary experiential sequence exists in all these works of the Holy Spirit. The experience of salvation is rightly called both a miracle and a mystery. An individual may associate particular aspects of the experience with certain times and places, but salvation is not something that can be programmed, nor is it finished in a particular moment at a particular place. Salvation is a work of the Holy Spirit which continues throughout the life of the believer on earth. It is not finally completed until the resurrection of the body at the end of the age, with the coming of Jesus the Messiah.

The first letter of Peter explores some of the complexity and richness of the experience of salvation, beginning with this description: "By his (God's) great mercy he has given us a new birth into a living hope through the resurrection of Jesus Christ from the dead, and into an inheritance that is imperishable, undefiled and unfading . . ." (1:3-4). Great mercy, new birth, living hope, resurrection of Jesus Christ, an inheritance that is imperishable—what richness!

1 Peter also describes this salvation as the outcome of faith (1:9), a continuing experience, something into which one grows. "Like newborn infants, long for the pure, spiritual milk, so that by it you may grow into salvation—if indeed you have tasted that the Lord is good" (2:2). Finally, the Epistle tells believers that salvation is an inheritance "kept in heaven for (them), . . . ready to be revealed in the last time" (1:4, 5). This statement recalls the words of Paul in the Roman letter, where he says that "the creation waits with eager longing for the revealing of the children of God" (8:19). In the meantime, Paul says, "We ourselves, who have the first fruits of the Spirit, groan inwardly while we wait for adoption, the redemption of our bodies" (8:23).

Particular dimensions of the salvation experience are the outcome of faith. These include sanctification, growth in grace, preservation of believers, and Christian assurance, all works of the Holy Spirit in the continuing experience of God's salvation in Jesus Christ. An inquiry into these works of the Holy Spirit will illuminate what it means to grow into salvation.

God Sanctifies Persons

Sanctification is an act by which God sets some thing or person apart for a divine purpose. That which God sets apart becomes, by God's act, sacred or holy. The descriptions of the furnishing of the Tabernacle in Exodus and Leviticus provide an example. The worship of God in the Tabernacle required the setting apart of particular vessels and other objects for special purposes. Through the rituals of sanctification performed by the priests, God set these furnishings apart. In these actions, these objects became sacred and holy.

In the original creation of the world, and in the creation of the human family in particular, God set all things apart for divine purposes. In this most basic sense, then, all of creation is sacred or holy. In a unique sense this is so for persons, because they are created in God's image. Included in their purpose were responsibilities for the care of the rest of creation. (See Gen. 1:26.)

Human sin and rebellion against God has compromised the sanctification of persons in their creation and corrupted the purpose for which God created them. Created for fellowship with God in a relationship of complete dependence, persons have rebelled against God and sought to take charge of their own destinies. Instead of receiving life daily and thankfully from the hands of God, they yielded to the deception that they could become gods themselves.

Violence of persons against persons immediately demonstrates the magnitude of this rebellion by creatures made in the divine image. Cain's murder of his brother Abel was a harbinger of the reckless and relentless desecration and destruction of persons by other persons throughout human history. Scripture regards these violations against the sacredness and holiness of persons as nothing less than a deliberate affront to the holy God. (See Gen. 9:6.)

The tragedy that resulted and continues to result from persons' inhumanity to other persons spreads to the rest of creation. Today's environmental crisis is one of the evidences of the impact of human sin on the rest of creation. The apostle Paul noted that the whole creation is groaning "from its bondage to decay [death]" (Rom 8:21, 22). The Confession puts it this way: "The alienation of persons from God affects the rest of creation, so that the whole creation stands in need of God's redemption" (2.06).

The Good News from Scripture is that through God's redemption, the sacredness of persons and of all of creation may be restored. The doctrine of sanctification deals with this restoration. By their new creation in the redemptive act of sanctification of persons God the Holy Spirit adds a new dimension of God's purpose for them.

This new dimension goes beyond daily fellowship with God, in which persons receive life daily from the hands of God. It goes beyond stewardship responsibilities for the rest of creation. The Confession puts it this way: "Sanctification is God's setting apart of believers as servants in the world" (4.21). Being God's servants in the world includes the responsibility to witness to the Gospel, and the expectation of service to people in need out of self-giving love.

Though believers are sanctified, set apart by God and called to live a holy life, their "struggle with sin continues" (COF 4.23). The Confession says plainly, "Believers never achieve sinless perfection in this life" (4.22). Elaborating on this continuing struggle, the Confession says, "Believers are still imperfect in knowledge and power to do God's will. Their freedom to trust, love and serve God and neighbors is compromised sometimes by distrust, hate, and selfishness" (4.23).

Scripture honestly faces the tension between sanctification and the continuing problem of sin. 1 John 3:9 states, "Those who have been born of God do not sin, because God's seed abides in them; they cannot sin because they are born of God." At the same time, a text in 1 John cautions believers, "If we say we have no sin, we deceive ourselves and the truth is not in us" (1:8). The Confession describes the process which gradually overcomes this tension as growth in grace.

Growth in Grace

The Confession states that, though believers never achieve sinless perfection in this life, "through the ministry of the Holy Spirit they can progressively be conformed to the image of Jesus Christ, thereby growing in faith, hope, love and other gifts of the Spirit" (4.22). In the Roman letter, Paul described the process by which persons are conformed to the image of Christ. "Brothers and sisters, by the mercies of God, . . . present your bodies (yourselves) as a living sacrifice, holy and acceptable to God, which is your spiritual worship. Do not be conformed to this world, but be transformed by the renewing of your minds, so that you may discern what is the will of God" (Rom. 12:1, 2).

Being "transformed by the renewing of your minds" is what Paul described in the letter to the Philippians as having "the same mind in you that was in Christ Jesus" (2:5). He went on to describe this mind of Christ as the mind of a servant, one who would be obedient to God "to the point of death—even death on a cross." This is what the Confession calls growing "in grace and the knowledge of Jesus Christ as Lord" (4.22).

The Confession describes the process of growing in grace as a struggle, "an inner struggle" that "drives [believers] again and again to rely on God's power to conform them to the image of the new person in Jesus Christ" (4.23). The apostle Paul had experienced the agony of this struggle. At one point in the Roman letter he cried out in desperation for deliverance from the struggle. He wrote, "for I delight in the law of God in my inmost self, but I see in my members another law at war with the law of my mind, making me captive to the law of sin that dwells in my members. Wretched man that I am! Who will rescue me from this body of death?" (7:22-24).

Confronted by this schizophrenic condition, Paul said honestly, "I do not understand my own actions. For I do not do what I want, but I do the very thing I hate. . . . I can will what is right, but I cannot do it" (Rom. 7:15, 19). In effect, Paul was saying that he was two persons, one which wanted to live according to the flesh and one which wanted to live according to the spirit. Paul's use of the terms flesh and spirit has sometimes been misunderstood as a reference to the physical body and the non-physical soul or spirit. A closer examination will show that the distinction he makes is between the old person, who is in bondage to sin and death, and the new person, who is resurrected with Christ. (See Rom. 6:1-11.)

Paul's letters to Christians in Ephesus and Colossae clearly demonstrate his distinction between the old and new selves. He reminds the Ephesians, "You were taught to put away your former way of life, your old self, corrupt and deluded by its lusts, and to be renewed in the spirit of your mind, and to clothe yourselves with the new self, created according to the likeness of God in true righteousness and holiness" (Eph. 4:22-24). This is the struggle with sin, which the Confession says continues throughout the earthly life of the believer.

Paul reminds the Christians at Colossae that they have "been raised with Christ," which should mean that they have died to sin. It was obvious , however, that they had not fully died to sin, for Paul urged them to put aside "the ways (they) . . . once followed," to "get rid of . . . anger, wrath, malice, slander, abusive language," and not to "lie to one another." (See Col. 3:1-9.) The letter states the reason for possibility of such behavior: "you have stripped off the old self with its practices and have clothed yourselves with the new self, which is being renewed in knowledge according to the image of its creator" (3:9 10).

These texts from Romans, Ephesians and Colossians indicate that the process of stripping off the old self and being clothed with the new self is what the Confession calls growing in grace. 1 Peter 2:2 calls this process "growing into salvation." In the Galatian letter, Paul described it as putting off the works of the flesh—"fornication, impurity, licentiousness, idolatry, sorcery, enmities, strife, jealousy, anger, quarrels, dissensions, factions, envy, drunkenness, carousing, and things like these," and living by the Spirit. Living by the Spirit brings the freedom for which God created persons and yields the fruit of the Spirit—"love, joy, peace, patience, kindness, generosity, faithfulness, gentleness, and self control." (See Gal. 5:16-24.)

Finally, growing in grace is the process by which the believer gradually becomes able to live according to grace. Living graciously means being set free from the bondage to self-love, self-centeredness, and receiving the "freedom to trust, love and serve God and neighbors" (COF 4:23). To live graciously is to have the mind of Christ, to be transformed according to the image of Christ.

Preservation of Believers

The description of the Christian life as a struggle to put off the old self and to become clothed in the new self understandably provokes questions about the ultimate outcome of the struggle. Believers personalize the questions in various ways: "How can I be sure that I can hold out to the end? Is there a danger that I may lose my salvation?" Scripture speaks to these questions, and the Confession summarizes its teachings in the section titled "Preservation of Believers." Such questions indicate either a misunderstanding of the nature of salvation or a lack of faith in God, or both.

One of the most common misunderstandings of the nature of salvation is that it is a joint work of God and the person, each doing a part. In an invitation to unbelievers following the sermon, a pastor may say, "God has already done his part. Now it is up to you to do your part." Some describe the situation as meeting God half way. The part done by the unbeliever usually includes repentance and faith, often embodied in the simple act of choosing Jesus.

The line of reasoning that follows from this understanding of salvation leads to this conclusion: If it is a joint work, then it must be jointly maintained. If and when the believer stops doing his or her part, salvation is put at risk. This is to make salvation a kind of hybrid, the result both of grace and law (works). Statements such as, "Salvation is of grace, but the person keeps it intact by obeying God's laws" reflect this understanding. This thinking can lead to further statements such as, "I don't see how that person can claim to be Christian and continue doing those things."

A second source of misunderstanding about the nature of salvation is its total identification with a particular religious experience. Particular and especially dramatic religious experiences are significant to the believer, and should be treasured. It is risky, however, to tie the authenticity of one's salvation to such an experience. Danger always exists that a particular religious experience will fade in intensity or become questionable. Salvation is a continuing experience, in which believers receive the grace and mercy of God every morning.

A third source of misunderstanding about the nature of salvation is in regarding it as something like a package one receives. Common comparisons of salvation with an insurance policy against the fires of hell or a ticket to the pleasures of heaven serve as examples of this misunderstanding. In fact, salvation is a present reality, not simply a guarantee concerning eternity. It is not a thing but a relationship with God, a relationship that comes from being a child of the family of God.

Uncertainty about one's salvation, for whatever reason, reflects a lack of faith and trust in God. If a weak faith puts one's salvation at risk, however, all believers have reason to be fearful. Scripture confirms the truth that the certainty of salvation depends on God, not the level of strength of the believer's faith. In fact, even faith is not something self-generated; it is a gift of God.

Faith, and all other aspects of salvation, are the work of God the Holy Spirit. This is the reason that Paul could say to the Philippian Christians, "I am confident of this, that the one who began a good work in you will bring it to completion by the day of Jesus Christ" (1:6). In an echo of Paul, the Confession says, "The transformation (salvation) of believers begun in regeneration and justification will be brought to completion. Although believers sin and thereby displease God, the covenant relationship is maintained by God, who will preserve them in eternal life" (4.24).

God's maintenance of the covenant relationship assures the preservation of believers. The covenant is not a covenant of law, which is maintained by a satisfactory performance of the works of the law by the person. Rather, it is a covenant of grace. Accordingly, the Confession says, "The preservation of believers depends on the nature of the covenant of grace, the unchangeable love and power of God, the merits, advocacy and intercession of Jesus Christ, and the presence and ministry of the Holy Spirit who renews God's image in believers" (4.25).

With this covenant of grace in mind, Paul asked, "Who can separate us from the love of Christ?" Answering his own question, Paul listed everything from hunger and lack of clothing to "any thing else in all creation," finally concluding that none of these things "will be able to separate us from the love of God in Christ Jesus." (See Rom. 8:35-39.) Indeed, even before God demonstrated the covenant of grace in the death and resurrection of Jesus Christ, Jesus had given witness to the preservation of believers. He said of those who hear and believe the Word, "I give them eternal life, and they will never perish. No one will snatch them out of my hand" (Jn. 10:28).

Christian Assurance

The certainty of one's salvation depends on what God does, not what the believer does or does not do. 2 Timothy 2:13 states, "If we are faithless, he (God in Christ) remains faithful—*for he cannot deny himself.*" (Italics added.) For God to do anything other than to preserve believers in eternal life would be for God to deny himself, to act in a manner that contradicts the covenant of grace and the very nature of God revealed in the life, death, and resurrection of Jesus the Christ.

There are times when believers are weak in faith, even faithless. The Confession confirms this and cautions that "assurance may not immediately accompany initial trust in Christ" (4.29). Initial trust, however dramatic the religious experience, should not be expected to give assurance of salvation for the rest of one's life. In the words of the Confession, this kind of assurance comes "as the believer faithfully participates in the worship, sacraments, ministry, witness, and life of the covenant community, through which God confirms to believers the promise never to leave nor forsake them" (4.29).

Another way of understanding how assurance comes to the believer is through the continuing presence of the Holy Spirit. As the Confession puts it, "This comforting assurance is founded upon . . . the witness of the Holy Spirit with the believers' spirits, that they truly are the children of God" (4.28). In the 8th chapter of Romans Paul explains how the Spirit of God in Christ dwells in believers, giving them continuing assurance as they live according to grace.

Paul says that the presence of the Spirit of God in Christ in persons distinguishes their new natures from their old, sinful natures (Rom. 8:1-8). When we pray to God as Father, "It is that very Spirit bearing witness with our Spirit that we are children of God" (8:16). What is more, even when we reach a point where our faith is so weak that we don't know how, or cannot pray, "that very Spirit intercedes with sighs too deep for words. . . . The Spirit intercedes for the saints according to the will of God" (8:27).

According to Paul, the Spirit of God bears witness to the spirit of believers that they are the children of God. Paul then points out some of the ramifications of being the children of God: "If children, then heirs, heirs of God and joint heirs with Christ" (Rom. 8:17). This recalls the discussion of Jesus with Nicodemus about how one enters the Kingdom of God, by being born of the Spirit. (See Jn. 3:1-10.) In fact, John 1:12 anticipates Jesus' explanation. That texts states that all who receive the Word made flesh, who believe in Jesus the Christ, will receive "power to become children of God."

Children are heirs. What they receive from their parents comes to them because they are children. With respect to the certainty of salvation, the Confession says, "Assurance is the promise of the believers' full inheritance" (4.28). For this reason it is misleading to ask unbelievers to choose Christ. One may choose to join an organization or a club, but the covenant community is not fundamentally an organization or a club. It is a family, the family of God. One does not choose to join, but is born or adopted into the family of God.

Understanding this fundamental distinction is critical to experiencing Christian assurance. In the last analysis, the security of a child resides in the love, care and protection of parents. With respect to eternal security, Paul's affirmation answers the questions of fearful believers. He says that nothing in all creation "will be able to separate us from the love of God in Christ Jesus our Lord" (Rom. 8:38-39).

Some object to and perhaps are fearful of the claim that God the Holy Spirit will preserve those who have been justified, regenerated and adopted into the family of God, assuring them of eternal salvation. They agree that persons are saved by grace, initially, but argue that such persons must work to retain their salvation. If they do not persevere, they are lost again. They fall from grace, and are bound for hell again. Some justify such a view on the grounds that to believe otherwise cuts the nerve of moral striving. The argument appears to be that people will be good only when threatened with ultimate punishment in hell for being bad. This view is simply an extension of understanding salvation as a joint effort—God and the person each doing a part. If believers don't continue to do their part, they lose their salvation. This amounts to saying that salvation comes in accordance with the covenant of grace, but remains a part of the Christian life in accordance with the covenant of law.

In his letter to the Galatians, Paul described this view of starting out with grace, then switching to law, as falling from grace back into law. Having been himself rescued from bondage to a religion of law and saved by grace, Paul was not about to build up again the very things he tore down. To do so, he argued, would be to "nullify the grace of God; for if justification [ultimately] comes through the law, then Christ died for nothing." (See Gal. 2:15-21.)

The sanctification of persons means that God sets them apart for a divine purpose. This occurs first in their creation. As defined in creation, their purpose is to worship and glorify God, receiving from God daily the gift of life; and to serve as stewards of the rest of creation. In their new creation by God the Holy Spirit, God gives persons the added purpose of being witnesses to others concerning God's salvation and of being God's servants to people who suffer in this world because of neglect, hatred, injustice and greed.

For Discussion

1. How do you react to the claim that sanctification, growth in grace, preservation of believers, and Christian assurance "do not come after salvation, but are dimensions of the continuing miracle and mystery of God's saving grace"?; that salvation "is a continuing work of the Holy Spirit throughout the life on earth of the believer," and is not "finally completed until the resurrection of the body at the end of the age"?
2. Identify specific examples of the ongoing process of sanctification in your life and in the life of those with whom you share experience in the covenant community. How valuable is it for you to understand sanctification as an ongoing, incomplete process?
3. What experiences in your own life can you discuss which match Paul's predicament when he said that he found himself doing exactly what he didn't want to do and not doing what he knew he should do? What resources are helpful to you as you deal with this continuing struggle between your two selves?
4. How might you respond to an earnest question from a friend outside our faith tradition about the possibility of falling from grace or losing faith?
5. How can you live in the confident assurance which the covenant of grace allows and not grow complacent and cease to grow? What resources challenge you to continue on your journey of faith?

CHAPTER 9

GOD CREATES THE CHURCH

Read Confession of Faith 3.03-3.04, 3.06, 3.09, 3.11, 5.01-5.11; Scriptures listed for these sections; and Constitution 1.1–2.01, 2.13.

Introduction

Many have referred to the events recorded in Acts 2 as the birthday of the church. Church bodies which refer to themselves as New Testament churches particularly reflect this view. Neither the Westminster Confession nor any one of the Cumberland Presbyterian revisions (1814, 1883, 1984) acknowledges a scriptural basis for such a view. All these confessions make the claim that the church is co-extensive with what the 1984 Cumberland Presbyterian Confession calls "the finished and continuing work of Christ" (5.03). Though this work "occurred at a particular time and place," its "powers and benefits extend to the believer *in all ages from the beginning of the world*" (COF 3.11, italics added).

God created the church in the world with the redemption of the first persons in Jesus Christ. If the church "is founded on the finished and continuing work of Christ," and if that redemptive work "extends to the believer in all ages from the beginning of the world," then the church has existed "from the beginning of the world."

Colossians 1:15-27 makes this claim in explicit terms, saying of Jesus the Christ, "He himself is before all things, and in him all things hold together. He is the head of the body, the church; he is the beginning, the firstborn from the dead, so that he might come to have first place in everything." The text goes on to describe this redemptive work of God in Jesus Christ as "the mystery that has been hidden throughout the ages and generations but has now been revealed to his saints."

Ephesians 2:19-20 calls the church the "household of God," and describes it as "built upon the foundation of the apostles and prophets, with Christ Jesus himself the chief cornerstone." Ephesians goes on to say that the deliberate inclusion of the Gentiles in the covenant community was always in God's plan. "The plan of the mystery hidden for ages in God" is now "made known to the rulers and authorities in the heavenly places." (See Eph. 3:9-10.)

It is about this "mystery hidden for ages" that the author of Hebrews speaks. He describes the faith response to God of persons beginning with Abel, and traces this faith community down through the ages. (See Heb. 11:1–12:2.) All these people have "died in faith without having received the promises, but from a distance they saw and greeted them" (Heb. 11:13). The writer of Hebrews says that "God is not ashamed to be called their God; indeed he has prepared a city for them" (11:16). What they saw from a distance and greeted was "Jesus the pioneer and perfecter of our faith" (Heb. 12:2).

God Creates the Covenant Community

In the act of the redemption of persons, God creates the covenant community, a family of persons bound to God both in creation and in redemption (the new creation). Accordingly the Confession affirms: "The church, as the covenant community of believers who are redeemed, includes all people in all ages, past, present, future, who respond in faith to God's covenant of grace, and all who are unable to respond, for reasons known to God, but who are saved by his grace" (5.06).

In the first eleven chapters of Genesis, which contains a generalized history of the beginnings of the human family, the covenant community does not appear as a particular historical body. There are references to particular persons of faith, but not to a faith community. The New Testament Letter to the Hebrews refers to Abel, Enoch, and Noah as persons of faith.

The generalized history of Genesis does, however, affirm certain articles of faith which provide the context for the story of God's redemption that unfolds in the history of the covenant community. These articles of faith include affirmations about God's creation of the human family, the rebellion and sin of the creatures made in the divine image, and the beginnings of God's work of redemption of sinful persons and of the world corrupted by their sin.

It is not until Genesis 12 that Scripture records the beginning of an identifiable historical community of redeemed people bound to God in the covenant of grace. This community originally consists of Abraham and Sarah and their family, and reaches forward into history to include all their descendants according to faith. (See Gen 12:1-3; 17:1-7; Gal. 3:6-9, 27-29; Heb. 11:8-40.)

Why did God choose a family of Hebrew people and their immediate blood descendants as the beginning of the covenant community? The Hebrews themselves asked that very question. In preparing the Israelites to go into the land of Canaan, Moses sought to create in their minds and hearts a profound sense of who God called them to be. Referring to God's covenant with Abraham and Sarah, and to the deliverance of their descendants from bondage in Egypt, Moses said, "Ask now about former ages, long before your own, ever since the day God created human beings on the earth; ask from one end of heaven to the other: has anything so great as this ever happened or has it ever been heard of?" (Deut. 4:32).

In the face of such a remarkable happening, the persistent question in the minds of devout, thankful believers was, "Why us?" Deuteronomy's answer involves the mystery of God's love. God did these things because of love, and out of faithfulness to the covenant with Abraham and Sarah. (See Deut. 7:6-8; 9:5.) This is the mystery of which the prophets had inquired, but which was to be revealed fully only in the birth, life, death and resurrection of Jesus Christ. It is the Christ event that offers final answers. This is the reason, in the language of the Confession, that the church is "founded on the *finished and continuing* work of Christ" (5.03 italics added).

The love of God shown to the world in Jesus Christ is a self-giving, suffering, redemptive love. It is no accident that Moses characterized God's creation of the covenant community in the call of Abraham and Sarah as an act of love, nor that the Hebrews came to understand their deliverance from bondage as an act of God's faithfulness to the covenant of grace made with Abraham and Sarah. As an act of redemptive love, the exodus was the re-creation or renewal of the covenant community, which foreshadowed God's mighty act of redemption in Jesus Christ to liberate the whole world from bondage to sin and death.

In the re-creation or renewal of the covenant community in the exodus, God defined more clearly the nature of the mission of that community. After emphasizing the event of their liberation from bondage, and after pointing out that the whole world and all its people belonged to God, Exodus 19:6 tells the Israelites, "You shall be to me a priestly kingdom and a holy nation." God set this community of people apart to be a community of priests to the whole world and to its people. From Exodus 19 to Malachi 4, the Old Testament is a story of how God worked to teach and lead Israel, forming the people into the servant community God called them to be.

Built on the Foundation of the Prophets

The land of Canaan was the geographical location in which God would form and teach the historical community of Israel to be the people of God. After arriving in the land of Canaan, the people of Israel began to distort what it meant for them to be chosen or called by God. They began to interpret chosen to mean that they and they alone were God's people. All other people became their actual or potential enemies, and therefore enemies of God. Second, they came to regard the land of Canaan as their property, where they would live throughout all time. In effect, the people of Israel converted their land and their ethnic identity into idols, and worshipped them instead of God. In their nationalistic idolatry, they lost sight of the mission in the world to which God had called them. Scripture clearly reflects these misunderstandings and distortions of the covenant.

However, God raised up prophets in Israel to call the people away from their worship of nation and land to the worship of God, who had delivered them from bondage into freedom. The prophets taught the people the meaning of the exodus, and how they were to live in thanksgiving for the grace God showed to them. The prophets taught the Hebrews what it meant to be faithful to the covenant of grace. It was the prophets who began to say that all people of the world were God's people, and who described Israel's mission as a light to the nations. It was the prophets who said that in the destruction of their national state and their removal to other lands, God was scattering them among the nations so that they might perform the mission to which God had called. Speaking of Moses, the prophet Hosea said, "By a prophet the Lord brought Israel up from Egypt, and by a prophet he [Israel] was guarded" (Hos. 12:13). Through the prophet Moses, God gave Israel the Torah [teachings], which was to be the foundation for their life as the people of God. The Torah defined their relationship to God as a worshipping community. The Torah also defined their relationships within the community and toward other peoples.

In accordance with the covenant God made with Abraham and Sarah, the Torah made clear that God expected the people of Israel to worship the true and only God. (See Ex. 36; 20:2-7.) God called them to be priests of God to the people of the nations, leading them to worship God and to become part of the covenant community. God commanded them, "You shall love the alien as yourself" (Lev. 19:33). God told the Hebrews to admit those aliens to the Passover who desired to claim God's mighty act in liberating Israel from bondage. "Any alien residing among you who wishes to keep the passover to the Lord shall do so according to the statute of the passover . . . ; you shall have one statute for both the resident alien and the native (Hebrew)" (Num. 9:14).

The prophet Amos emphasized both God's lordship over all peoples (1:1; 2:3), and the covenant relationship which God had established with Israel. As a mouthpiece for God, Amos said, "You only have I known of all the families of the earth" (Am. 3:2). The divine lordship over all nations meant that God in some sense "knew them." In speaking of Israel, however, the phrase translated "have known" referred to the kind of intimate, personal knowledge that is characteristic of the relationship between a husband and a wife. This was the covenant relationship. The prophet Hosea would later make explicit use of the marriage metaphor to describe the covenant relationship between God and Israel.

The prophecy of Amos contains other ideas that also became part of the prophetic foundation of the covenant community. Amos raised the prospect of Israel's destruction as a national state, and the resettlement of Israelites in other lands. (See 3:9-11; 4:1-3.) In this context, Amos introduced the concept of the remnant, a means by which to distinguish those Israelites who remained faithful to the covenant from those who were simply descendants of Abraham and Sarah according to the flesh. The prophecy of Amos contains two other affirmations that constitute part of the prophetic foundation of the church. The prophet not only asserted God's lordship over other nations; he claimed that in some particular sense God's providence was over each ethnic group (Am. 9:7). Finally, the book of Amos contains the first explicit reference to the ultimate fulfillment of God's purpose for the covenant community and for the whole creation in the coming of the Messiah and the messianic age (Am. 9:11-15).

The other great prophets, Isaiah, Micah, Jeremiah and Ezekiel elaborated on the themes Amos and Hosea had introduced, firmly establishing the prophetic foundation of the covenant community. Isaiah and Micah witnessed the destruction of northern Israel, and Assyria's deportation of thousands of Israelites to many regions throughout the Assyrian empire. Jeremiah and Ezekiel witnessed the destruction of Judah, the last remnant of the national state, and the deportation/exile of thousands of Israelites into Babylon.

Understandably, these blows to the ethnic and geographic idols, which a majority of Israelites had come to worship, created widespread despair. Addressing this loss of faith, one prophet of the exile asserted that the events which had transpired were in no way a sign of the impotence of the God of Israel. "Have you not known? Have you not heard? The Lord is the everlasting God, the creator of the ends of the earth. He does not faint or grow weary; his understanding is unsearchable" (Isa. 40:28).

Jeremiah had his own message to the fearful exiles in Babylon. He quoted God saying, "I will make an everlasting covenant with [Israel], never to draw back from doing good to them; and I will put the fear of me in their hearts, so that they may not turn from me" (Jer. 32:40). Ezekiel, in a dramatic vision, affirmed that the devastation left in the wake of the Babylonian exile did not mean the end of the covenant community. In this vision Ezekiel saw a valley of dry bones, and heard these words from God: "I will cause breath to enter you, and you shall live. . . . You shall know that I am the Lord" (Ez. 37:5-6).

The prophets not only laid the foundation on which the covenant community would continue, even with its members scattered among the nations, but they also began to stress its role as God's servant and witness to the nations. They began a radical transformation of the messianic hope, changing the concept of the Messiah from a military, political ruler into a servant. The prophets understood the messianic age not as a restoration of the national state of Israel, but as the consummation of God's purpose for the whole creation, involving people of all nations.

To Israel in exile, God said,"I have given you as a covenant to the people, a light to the nations, to open the eyes that are blind, to bring out the prisoners from the dungeon, and from prison those who sit in darkness" (Isa. 42:6-7; see also 61:1-3.) Through the Israelites, God extended the covenant to the peoples of the nations. God, through the prophets used the description of people as blind, sitting in prison and in darkness to help the Hebrews to recall their own circumstances in slavery in Egypt, from which God had set them free.

The story of Jonah and his unwilling witness to the Assyrians in the city of Nineveh serves both as a judgment on any continuing ethnic exclusiveness on the part of the Israelites and as a promise of what the future held for the covenant community as a witness to the nations. Jesus would later reprimand the religious leaders of Jerusalem for not understanding the sign of Jonah. (See Lu. 1:29-32.)

The prophetic transformation of the concepts of the covenant community and the coming of the messianic age were no less radical than the transformation of the concept of the Messiah itself. The Messiah, as "a shoot . . . from the stump of Jesse," (Isaiah 11:1) would be a servant Lord. He would not appear in splendor as did the kings of the earth. In fact, he would be "despised and rejected" by many, and be "held . . . of no account." The most radical claim of all was that this servant Messiah would rule by bearing the sins of the whole world, pouring "out himself to death." (See Isa. 53:1-12.) The covenant community, the church, was "built upon the foundation of . . . the prophets, with Christ (Messiah) Jesus himself as the cornerstone" (Eph. 2:20).

The Body of Christ

The church is the covenant community, created by God in the covenant with Abraham and Sarah and established on the foundation of the prophets. It has been "founded on the finished and continuing work of Christ" (COF 5.03). With respect to that continuing work, Scripture speaks of the church as the body of Christ. The metaphor of the church as the body of Christ is what Ephesians 5:32 calls "a great mystery." The church is not simply a body of people, an organization, or even a community. It is Christ's body. In the words of the Confession: "There is one, holy, universal, apostolic church. She is the body of Christ, who is her Head and Lord" (5.01).

In the New Testament, the Greek word translated body is soma. When used in reference to a person, it often means not simply the physical body but the whole person. In Romans 12:1, Paul urged, "Brothers and sisters, by the mercies of God, . . . present your bodies (yourselves) as a living sacrifice, holy and acceptable to God." Paul goes on to use this same term as a metaphor for the church. This means that as a body, the church is essentially personal in nature. It is not simply an organization, but a living, growing organism.

The source of this Pauline concept may have been the words of Jesus himself in the institution of the Lord's Supper. Paul was certainly familiar with the words of the institution, as indicated by 1 Corinthians 11:23-34. In passing on this tradition, Paul emphasized the importance of discerning the Lord's body, when eating the bread and drinking the cup. Earlier in this letter, Paul had said explicitly that in eating the bread and drinking the cup, believers are "sharing in the body of Christ" (See 10:15-17.) Paul certainly meant sharing in Christ, not simply in a physical body of a man named Jesus.

The mystery of how believers share in the body of Christ, or become the body of Christ, is the focus of Paul's discussion of how persons who are dead in sin are resurrected to new life in Christ. (See Romans 5:12-6:14). After describing the universal human predicament of bondage to sin and death, Paul pinpointed the death and resurrection of Jesus Christ as the only hope. To be united with Christ in a death like his means that the body (person) of sin is destroyed. This is what occurred on the Cross. Paul continued: "But if we have died with Christ, we believe that we shall also live with him." Believers find themselves united with Christ in his resurrection. Speaking to believers, Paul said, "So you also must consider yourselves dead to sin and alive to God *in Christ Jesus*. (Italics added).

The church, as the body of Christ, consists of persons with whom

Christ has died the death of sin on the Cross, and who have experienced resurrection from death to life through the rising of Christ. The church is where persons may and do encounter the risen Lord. The church is a kind of continuation of the incarnation of Christ in the world, where the risen Christ still has a human face. It is a fellowship of persons in which the risen Christ appears incognita, as on the road to Emmaus, or behind locked doors, only to be recognized by faith.

The letters to the Ephesians and the Colossians develop the metaphor of the church as the body of Christ and include references to Christ as head of the body. The Ephesian letter admonishes, "We must grow up in every way into him who is the head, into Christ, from whom the whole body is joined and knit together. . ." (Eph. 4:15). The Colossian letter states, "[Christ] is the head of the body, the church; he is the beginning of the firstborn from the dead . . . For in him all the fullness of God was pleased to dwell . . ." (Col. 1:18-19). The scripture uses the body metaphor repeatedly, especially when it identifies Christ as the head of the body, to stress both the unity and diversity of the church. The body has many members, which points to the diversity of gifts in the church. Christ, as the head of the body, is the source of the unity of the church. (See Rom. 12:3-8; I Cor. 12:1-31; Eph. 4:1-32.)

The Apostolic Church

The Confession of Faith says, "The church is apostolic because God calls her into being through the proclamation of the gospel first entrusted to the apostles" (5.05). The Confession goes on to interpret this to mean that the church is "built on the apostolic message which is faithfully proclaimed by messengers who follow in the footsteps of the apostles." This is in keeping with the claim of Ephesians 2:19-20, that the "household of God" is "built on the foundation of the apostles and prophets, with Christ Jesus himself as the cornerstone." See Eph. 3:5; 4:11; Isa. 28:16; Mt. 16:19; 21:42.)

Understanding the nature of the church requires a grasp and appreciation of the sense in which it is apostolic, built on the apostles and on the continuing witness to the apostolic tradition. Considerable dispute exists about the meaning of Jesus' statement to Peter: "I tell you, you are Peter, and on this rock I will build my church, and the gates of hell will not prevail against it" (Mt. 16:18). Ephesians 2:19-20 claims that the church is built on the foundation of the apostles. Peter, then, becomes the spokesman for the apostles and shares with them as the foundation of the church.

Taken together, the Ephesian text and Acts 2 can present an argument that the church is a New Testament church. This position, however, overlooks the claim that the church was also built on the foundation of the prophets. Such a position also ignores Paul's claim in Galatians 3:1-9, 29 about the continuity of the faith community all the way to Abraham. It also fails to consider the picture given in Hebrews 11:1–12:2, which extends this faith community back to Abel. The Confession claims that the church is universal in time as well as place. This is so because though "God's work of reconciliation in Jesus Christ occurred at a particular time and place, . . . its benefits extend to believers in all ages from the beginning of the world" (COF 3.11).

In essence, the significance of the apostolic foundation parallels the prophetic foundation. The prophets gave definitive shape to the meaning of the exodus event, describing it as God's effort to fashion, lead and discipline the covenant community. (See Deut. 18:18-19.) The prophets were incomparable interpreters of the covenant of grace. They always prefaced their messages with a call to the Israelites to remember that once they were aliens (no people), in bondage in Egypt, but that by a mighty act of salvation God made them into a people, the covenant people.

Just as the prophets were the authoritative interpreters of the exodus event, laying a foundation on which the church was and is being built, so the apostles served as the authoritative interpreters of the Christ event, building on the foundation on which the church was and is being built. The Lord's Supper dramatizes the continuity of the apostolic witness with the prophetic witness. As the passover celebrated God's salvation of Israel in the exodus, so the Lord's Supper celebrates God's salvation of the whole world in Jesus the Christ.

An apostle is someone who is sent out on a mission, an individual authorized to act on behalf of the sender. Governments commonly used the term in reference to a representative of one government to another, as in the case of messengers or ambassadors. The Gospel uses the term to refer to the twelve disciples whom Jesus sent out on a mission, as messengers of the Kingdom of God. (See Lu. 9:1-6.)

The unique and authoritative role of the Twelve in laying a foundation for the church derives from the particular relationship they shared with Jesus the Messiah. In this relationship they experienced the most intimate moments of the ministry of Jesus, received teachings from Jesus from the earliest days of his ministry, observed his healing ministry, and were witnesses to his death and resurrection.

Acts 1:15-16, giving details of choosing a replacement for Judas Iscariot, confirms the unique and authoritative role of the Twelve. Peter appears to have presided over a meeting of 120 believers to elect a successor to Judas, and to have laid down the qualifications of a candidate. The person replacing Judas must have been in the company of disciples from the beginning of the ministry of Jesus and must have been a witness to the Resurrection. On the basis of the account, the number of persons who met these qualifications is unknown, but two names were placed in nomination. The group elected a man named Matthias.

Despite the unique and authoritative role of the Twelve, the Gospels, Acts, and I Corinthians all contain evidence that the concept of apostolic authority was not confined to them. Paul refers to himself and Barnabas as apostles. (1 Cor. 9:3-6). He spoke of a resurrection appearance to "more than five hundred brothers and sisters at one time," then to James and "all the apostles," and finally to Paul himself. (See 1 Cor. 15:3-8.)

Though it may be difficult, within the limits of the New Testament, to determine the exact number of apostles, it is clear that certain characteristics were prerequisites. In general terms, one must have been an eyewitness to the Christ event. The exact scope of the required firsthand knowledge is uncertain, but it is clear that having been a witness to the resurrection of Jesus the Christ was absolutely essential. It is probable that those who attacked Paul's claim to apostolic authority did so on the grounds that he had an insufficient firsthand knowledge of the Christ event. (See Gal. 1:13-24.)

Shortly before his ascension into heaven, Jesus himself established the critical role of the apostolic witness. He said to the eleven apostles, "You will receive power when the Holy Spirit has come upon you; and you will be my witnesses in Jerusalem, in all Judea and Samaria, and to the ends of the earth" (Acts 1:8). The first example of this apostolic witness was the message Peter gave on the Day of Pentecost. Later when Peter and the other apostles appeared before the authorities in Jerusalem, they received "strict orders not to teach in (Jesus') name." They responded, "We must obey God rather than any human authority. . . . We are witnesses to these things." (See Acts 5:27-32.)

It is clear from the events recorded in Acts, that certain persons from among the eyewitnesses became authoritative sources of what Jesus the Christ had said and done. Equally if not more important, these particular persons were able to interpret the meaning of the Christ event from the Law and the Prophets. In particular, they grasped the meaning of his death and resurrection. It is for this reason that the teachings of these apostles, along with the prophets, became the foundation of the church.

The pastoral and general epistles contain evidence that false teachings began to be a problem in the church relatively early. In these situations, the apostolic witness played a critical role in shaping the proclamation of the Gospel. Instructions from 2 Peter serve as an example. After appropriate warnings about "false teachers..., who will secretly bring destructive opinions," the letter instructs its readers to "remember the words spoken in the past by the holy prophets, and the commandments of the Lord and Savior spoken through your apostles." (See 2 Pet. 2:1-3; 3:1-2.) The first epistle of John begins with these words: "We declare to you what was from the beginning, what we have heard, what we have seen with our eyes, what we have looked at and touched with our hands, concerning the word of life" (1 Jn. 1:1).

The Cumberland Presbyterian Church, and Protestantism in general, teaches that the apostolic office ended with the death of the generation of eyewitnesses of the Christ event. Nevertheless, the church is still being built on the apostolic foundation whenever and wherever its pastors and teachers remember "the commandments of the Lord and Savior spoken through (the) apostles." In the words of the Confession: "The church thus is built on the apostolic message which is faithfully proclaimed by messengers who follow in the footsteps of the apostles" (5.05).

The church, created by God, built on the foundations of the prophets and apostles, founded on the finished and continuing work of Christ "never exists for herself alone, but to glorify God" (COF 5.09). This means that God called the church into being and bound it in the covenant of grace as a community that worships God, and only God.

For Discussion

1. What is this "work of Christ," and in what sense is it both "finished and continuing"? Why is it important to claim that the church exists together with this "finished and continuing work of Christ"?
2. From your reading of Scripture, why did God initially call the church into being out of the ethnic group of people known as the Hebrews? Look specifically at Exodus 19:6.
3. What does it mean to you that the church is built on the foundation of the prophets and apostles?
4. What is the significance of the claim that the church is God's creation? How does this agree or differ with understandings of the church you may hold or hear?
5. If the church is the body of Christ in the world, the presence of Christ the world experiences, how might the church respond to:
    a. poverty, both rural or urban?
    b. violence between individuals and/or nations?
    c. chemical addiction and all of its related issues?

CHAPTER 10

THE CHURCH WORSHIPS GOD

Read Confession of Faith 5.12-5.27; 6.23-24 and Scriptures listed for these sections.

Introduction

The message which God gave through Moses to the Pharaoh of Egypt was, "Let my son [Israel] go, so that he may worship me" (Ex. 4:23). This message was repeated seven times before Pharaoh summoned Moses and Aaron in the night and said, "Rise up, go away from my people, both you and the Israelites! Go, worship the Lord, as you said." (See Ex. 5:1; 7:16; 8:1, 20; 9:1, 13; 10:3; 12:5.) At one point Pharaoh had said, "Go sacrifice to your God within the land" (Ex. 8:25). Moses responded, "If we offer in the sight of the Egyptians sacrifices that are offensive to them, will they not stone us?" (Ex. 8:26).

These texts reveal two things. First, God calls the covenant people out from among the rest of the population to be a worshipping community. Second, the fact that a community of people withdraws to worship God may be offensive to the rest of the population. Being called out to worship God means, in some sense, opposition to the world. God called the community of faith to become "a priestly kingdom and a holy nation" (Ex. 19:6). Such a role clearly was not possible for them under the conditions of slavery in Egypt.

Worship is the first vocation (calling) the people of the covenant community have from God. They serve God in worship. It is no accident, then, that the church refers to a worship event as a worship service. Acts of worship such as prayers, hymns, and offerings comprise a liturgy, a term derived from a Greek word meaning service. Neither is it an accident that the first two commandments the people of Israel received at Mt. Sinai bind them unequivocally to God in worship. (See Ex. 20:1-6). The concept of a people bound to God in a vocation of worship continues throughout the Old Testament and into the New Testament.

Jesus began his ministry by teaching in the synagogues (places of worship) of Galilee. (See Mk. 1:21, 39.) The disciples of Jesus were so profoundly influenced by his worship of God in prayer that they asked him to teach them how to pray (Lu. 11:1). On Pentecost, the three thousand who responded in repentance and faith to the Good News of the resurrection of Jesus the Messiah which Peter proclaimed "devoted themselves to the apostles' teaching and fellowship, to the breaking of bread and the prayers" (Acts 2:42). In Acts 3:1, Peter and John went "up to the Temple at the hour of prayer, at three o'clock in the afternoon." Clearly, Jesus and his followers continued the service to God in worship that had characterized the covenant community since the Exodus.

It was at services of worship in synagogues throughout Asia Minor and Greece that Paul proclaimed the Good News of the Resurrection of Jesus the Messiah. (See Acts 13:5, 14; 14:1; 17:1; 18:4.) The entire book of Hebrews offers an explanation of how the life, death and resurrection of Jesus the Messiah revolutionized the worship of the covenant community. Finally, the last scene pictured in the book of Revelation is of the church, the Bride of Christ, gathered before the throne of God worshipping God forever and ever. (Rev. 21:22–22:5). The Confession of Faith affirms that Christian worship "is central to the life of the church and is the appropriate response of all believers to the lordship and sovereignty of God" (5.12).

Worship on the Lord's Day

The practice of gathering one day each week for "the affirmation of God's living presence and the celebration of God's mighty acts" is at the heart of the worship of the covenant community in both the Old and New Testaments (COF 5.12; 6.23). In both the Old and New Testaments, the community gathered for worship on the Lord's Day, God's day. In the Old Testament, it was a celebration of God's creation of all things, hence it was observed on the seventh day, the Sabbath.

The rationale for the Sabbath given in Exodus 20:8-11 is that God rested on the seventh day following six days of work in the creation. "Therefore the Lord blessed the sabbath day and consecrated it" (Ex. 20:11). A parallel text in Deut. 5:12-15 gives a different rationale. This texts tells the Israelites, "Remember that you were a slave in the land of Egypt, and the Lord your God brought you out from there with a mighty hand and an outstretched arm" (Deut 5:15).

These two texts say that God consecrated the seventh day, setting it aside for a divine purpose. Keeping the Sabbath holy meant demonstrating respect for this divine purpose. Taken together, the texts suggest that God intended the Sabbath to be a time to remember and celebrate God's mighty act in the creation of the world *and* God's mighty act in the liberation of Israel from bondage in Egypt. These twin themes, creation and redemption, dominate the Old Testament. They become central to the worship of the covenant community in its great religious festivals and in its weekly observance of the Sabbath.

As the Confession of Faith notes, whether the seventh or the first, the day has always been the Lord's Day. "From the beginning of the world to the resurrection of Christ the seventh day of the week, known as the sabbath, was the Lord's Day. Subsequent to Christ's resurrection, Christians celebrate the first day of the week as the Lord's Day" (COF 6.23). Deuteronomy 5:14 says, "But the seventh day is a *sabbath to the Lord your God.*" (Italics added.) In Revelation 1:10, John spoke of *"being in the spirit on the Lord's day."* (Italics added.)

The resurrection of Christ was the reason for the change from the seventh to the first day of the week. However, nowhere in the New Testament is this change explained in a direct, explicit manner. It is inferred from claims made by Jesus that he came to fulfill the Law and the Prophets. (See Mt. 5:17. Jesus fulfilled the Passover by transforming it into the Lord's Supper. In a like manner, he fulfilled the Sabbath, a celebration of the creation of the world and the redemption of the people who constituted the covenant community, in the celebration of the new creation of all things through their redemption in his resurrection.

Speaking of Jesus as the new high priest, the writer of Hebrews said, "When there is a change in the priesthood, there is necessarily a change in the law as well" (Heb. 7:12). The change was in order because "the law has only a shadow of the good things to come and not the true form of these realities"(Heb. 10:1). Changing from the terminology of law to the that of the covenant, the writer of Hebrews said, "Jesus has now obtained a more excellent ministry, and to that degree he is the mediator of a better covenant, which has been enacted through better promises" (Heb. 8:6).

The difference in the first and the better covenant was not one of substance but of degree. Both were covenants of grace. The first was partial; the second was complete. In the words of the Confession, "Jesus Christ, the eternal word made flesh, is always the essence of the one covenant of grace. Before Christ's coming, it was made effective by promises, prophecies, sacrifices, circumcision, the passover lamb, and other signs and ordinances delivered to the people of Israel" (COF 3.04).

As Hebrews 8:7 observes, "If the first covenant had been faultless, there would have been no need to look for a second one." In the matter of the reconciliation of sinners to God, the blood of an animal was a shadow of the reality, God's own blood shed on Calvary in the death of Jesus the Christ. In a similar way, and for a similar reason, the Lord's

Day changed from the seventh to the first day as a means of replacing shadow with reality.

The seventh day of the week marked the completion of God's first creation. The first day of the week marked the completion of God's new creation through the resurrection of Jesus the Christ. Colossians 1:18-20 states that Jesus the Christ "is the beginning, the first born from the dead, that he might come to have first place in everything for in him all the fullness of God was pleased to dwell, and through him God was pleased to reconcile to himself all things, whether on earth or in heaven, by making peace through the blood of the cross."

The first New Testament indication of the centrality of the resurrection of Jesus the Christ in the divine drama of redemption and its impact on the day of worship appears in Acts 2. Pentecost occurred on the fiftieth day, the day following the seventh Sabbath after Passover. It is no accident, then, that when the followers of Jesus gathered together, the Holy Spirit fell upon them. The heart of Peter's message on that first day of the week was the Good News of the Resurrection. "Jesus of Nazareth, a man attested to you by God with deeds of power, wonders, and signs that God did through him among you, . . . you crucified and killed by the hands of those outside the law. *But God raised him up, having freed him from death, because it was impossible for him to be held in its power*" (Acts 2:22-24, italics added).

Though the followers of Jesus continued to worship in the Temple and in synagogues on the Sabbath, they also began to meet together on the first day of the week for the breaking of bread and for prayer. The prototype of this kind of fellowship and worship on the first day of the week may have been the experience of Jesus and the two disciples on the road to Emmaus on the day of his resurrection. (See Lu. 24:13-32.)

Paul was most influential in the change of the Lord's Day from the seventh to the first day of the week. Acts 20:7 is a clear indication that a meeting on the first day had become common practice for Paul. Paul's instructions concerning the offering to be taken for the saints in Jerusalem confirms this practice: "On the first day of every week, each of you should put aside and save whatever extra you earn . . ." (1 Cor. 16:2).

Inquiry into the change from the seventh to the first day emphasizes the importance of this day to the vocation of the covenant community to worship God. The Confession of Faith says that the Lord's Day is a time not only to reflect on and to celebrate God's mighty acts in creation and redemption, but also to affirm "God's living presence" and to reflect on "God's nature" (5.12, 6.23). In the Old Testament, the ark of the covenant, housed first in the tent of meeting (tabernacle) and later in the temple, signified the living presence of God. The ark of the covenant and the tent of meeting give important insights into the nature and presence of God (Ex. 25:10-22).

First, the ark, God's seat in the tent of meeting, was the ark of the covenant because God is a covenant-making God. The ark of the covenant recalls both God's covenant with Abraham and Sarah and their descendants and God's act of salvation in the exodus event. For this reason, Exodus 31:16 states, "Therefore the Israelites shall keep the sabbath, observing the sabbath throughout their generations as a *perpetual covenant*" (Ex. 31:16 italics added.)

The New Testament reveals that the covenant-making God became incarnate in Jesus the Messiah. The Confession of Faith says, "In worship God claims persons in Christ and offers assurance of love, forgiveness, guidance and redemption" (5.13). For the believer, the Lord's Day becomes a time to reflect on the nature of God and to celebrate God's covenant of grace in Jesus Christ.

Second, the community named the tent which housed the ark of the covenant the tent of meeting because this is where God met with the covenant community. The God Israel worshipped was not remote, remaining far off in heaven. The living, personal God lived in the midst of the covenant community. After giving Moses the instructions about the tent of meeting, God said, "I will meet with the Israelites there. . . . I will dwell among the Israelites, and I will be their God" (Ex. 29:43, 45).

The New Testament gives witness to the living presence of God in Jesus the Christ. Gathering to worship on the Lord's Day in the name of Christ is an affirmation of the living presence of God who raised Christ from the dead.

Worship of the gathered covenant community on the first day of the week "is central to the life of the church and is the appropriate response of all believers to the lordship and sovereignty of God" (COF 5.12). The Confession goes on to say, "This common worship of the church validates and sustains such other worship" as may be "practiced in various settings, especially in the home by individuals and by the family" (5.14, 5.15).

In describing this common, corporate worship of the covenant community, the Confession of Faith lists first the proclamation of the gospel of Jesus Christ. Since the resurrection of Jesus the Christ is at the heart of the Good News, and is the primary reason for worship on the first day of the week, then every Lord's Day should be a celebration of the Resurrection.

Worship and the Lord's Supper

In listing the components of public worship, the Confession of Faith ranks the sacraments second, after the proclamation of the Gospel of Jesus Christ. The "sacraments are signs and testimonies of God's covenant of grace," (COF 5.16) and they therefore present visibly the very heart of the gospel that has been proclaimed orally. Throughout its early history the Christian church universally observed Sunday with worship that included the celebration of the Lord's Supper. Both Luther and Calvin believed that the service of worship on the Lord's Day should always include the oral proclamation of the Gospel and its visible presentation in the Eucharist.

This is the current practice of Lutheran churches, which evolved from Luther's leadership, as well as the various branches of the Church of England and the Roman Catholic Church. These three branches of the church constitute the majority of Christians. Presbyterian and other Reformed churches did not follow Calvin's views on the celebration of the Lord's Supper; nor do most of the various segments of the Anabaptist and free church traditions celebrate the Lord's Supper every Lord's Day. In these traditions the celebration ranges from two or three times per year to once every month.

In fulfilling the Law and the Prophets the Christ event influenced the change of the celebration of the Lord's Day from the seventh to the first day of the week. A similar transformation occurred when Jesus' celebration of the Passover with his disciples led to the institution of the Lord's Supper. As in the case of the Lord's Day, this change recognizes both continuity with the old and the significance of the new.

The Passover celebrated God's mighty act of salvation of the people of Israel from bondage in Egypt and their creation as the covenant community. It was a family celebration, in the context of a family meal, and it included a recitation of God's mighty acts of redemption. It is no accident that Jesus instituted the Lord's Supper in the context of the celebration of Passover. Anticipating the events that were to occur, Jesus transformed the Passover into the Lord's Supper as a dramatic portrayal and embodiment of the mighty acts of God's salvation of the whole world.

The three terms used to refer to this sacrament, Communion, Eucharist, and Lord's Supper, all derive from Scripture; however, only the "Lord's Supper" actually occurs in Scripture (1 Cor. 11:20). The term Eucharist derives from a Greek word meaning "to give thanks." In its verb form, this is the word Jesus used at the passover meal with his disciples, when "he took a cup, and after giving thanks, he gave it to them" (Mt. 26:27; Mk 14:23; Lu. 22:17). Luke reports that Jesus used the same term after taking a loaf of bread(Lu. 22:19). Paul used the same term In reporting this tradition in 1 Corinthians 11:24.

The term Communion derives from the fellowship character of the event and its association with a fellowship meal. Indeed, its institution was in the context of the Passover, which was both a religious ritual and a family fellowship meal. Paul's report of the tradition of the Lord's Supper in 1 Corinthians 11:17-34 clearly shows its association with a fellowship meal.

Earlier in the Corinthian letter, Paul had described the Lord's Supper as an experience of sharing in the body of Christ, a phrase he often used to express the unity of the fellowship of believers. This association of the Lord's Supper with a fellowship meal may have grown out of the resurrection appearances of Jesus, which often occurred in the context of a meal with his followers. This may have contributed, also, to the festive character of the event. (See Lu. 24:28-43; Jn. 20:9-14; Acts 10:39-41.)

The Confession of Faith describes the sacraments as "signs and testimonies of God's covenant of grace" (5.16). This is particularly evident in the Lord's Supper, which focuses attention on the death and resurrection of Jesus the Christ. Its celebration is a proclamation of the suffering, self-giving love of God in Jesus Christ for rebellious sinners. It is an affirmation of the resurrection of Jesus Christ from bondage to the powers of death, by which sinners may be delivered from that bondage.

Jesus himself made the association of the Lord's Supper with his death in the institution of the sacrament. The bread is a sign or symbol of his body. The term body refers to the whole person, not simply to the physical body. In giving the disciples the bread, Jesus was giving himself to and for them in his death on the Cross.

Bread is also a symbol of life, which only God can give. According to John 6:48-59, Jesus referred to himself as the "bread of life," and drew a comparison between this bread and the manna which God gave the Israelites in the wilderness. Paul would later say that when the Israelites ate manna in the wilderness, they were actually eating "the same spiritual food" that is represented in the bread of the Eucharist.(See 1 Cor. 10:1-4.)

When Jesus gave the bread to his disciples saying, "This is my body, given for you," he meant "I am the bread of life. . . . Whoever eats me will live because of me" (Jn. 6:48, 57). In this sense, the bread does not point to the death of Jesus, but to his life. In his own words, "I am the *living bread* come down from heaven" (Jn. 6:51, italics added).

All the synoptic gospels report that when Jesus took the cup, he said that it was the covenant in his blood. In Luke 22:20, Jesus called it "the new covenant in my blood." The cup refers to the death of Jesus on the cross, a death that gives life. Just as the body of Christ is the bread of life, so also the blood of Jesus Christ is the drink of life. Thus Jesus said, "Those who eat my flesh and drink my blood have eternal life, and I will raise them up on the last day; for my flesh is true food and my blood is true drink" (Jn. 6:54, 55).

The Hebrew understanding that life itself resides in the blood illuminates the full impact of this reference to the blood of Jesus as the drink of life. The book of Leviticus reflects this understanding in its provisions for the shedding of the blood of an animal as a sacrifice to God. The Book of Hebrews fully explores this ritual and interprets it in relation to the death of Jesus Christ.

In Mt. 26:27-28 when Jesus took the cup he said, "Drink from it, all of you; for this is my blood of the covenant, which is poured out for many for the forgiveness of sins." The covenant to which Jesus referred is the covenant of grace, not a covenant of law. The death of Christ is a manifestation of God's grace, not a satisfaction of the penalty of the law. The key that unlocks this understanding is the knowledge that "without the shedding of blood there is no forgiveness of sin" (Heb. 9:22). That is, without the giving of life, there can be no new life.

Humans live in bondage to sin, alienated from God, and the cost of their reconciliation is very great. Indeed, any time a person is alienated from another person, the cost of reconciliation is great. The one at fault cannot bring about reconciliation by his own effort. It can come only as a gift, an act of self-giving love, from the one who has been wronged.

Reconciliation is not a gift if the one against whom wrong has been committed says, "If you will beg my forgiveness, and promise to do better, then I will forgive you." That is a bargain, a deal. Reconciliation is a gift only when the person who has been wronged says, unconditionally, "I forgive you." The one who forgives pours herself or himself out, as an act of self-giving love, to accomplish reconciliation. God in Jesus Christ poured himself out, shed his blood on the cross, to reconcile sinful persons to God.

Still another approach to this mystery of God's grace manifested in Jesus Christ is to appropriate in a more direct way the symbolism of the cup in the Lord's Supper. The Hebrew understanding was that life existed in the blood. Accordingly, Jesus said, "Very truly, I tell you, unless you eat the flesh of the Son of Man and *drink his blood,* you have no life in you" (Jn 6:53 italics added.) Modern medical procedures which transfer one person's blood to another powerfully demonstrate this symbolism. Life literally is in the blood.

Though the Lord's Supper is a remembrance of the death of Christ, it is not a celebration of his death. It is a celebration of the new life made possible through his resurrection. It is not the dead Christ who is present in the Lord's Supper, but the resurrected, living Christ. The Good News of the Resurrection makes the Lord's Supper a celebration. The Confession of Faith says, that the Lord's Supper "is a means by which the church remembers and shows forth Christ's passion and death on the cross," but it continues with the claim that it is a way "to celebrate and experience the continuing presence of the risen Lord" (5.23).

The Lord's Day changed from the seventh to the first day of the week because of the centrality of the Good News of the resurrection of Jesus the Christ. For the same reason, the celebration of the Lord's Supper on the Lord's Day is a celebration of the presence of the risen Lord. It is a remembrance of his death, but a celebration of his resurrection. This may explain how in the early church, the Lord's Supper became an integral part of public worship on the Lord's Day, the day of Resurrection.

Worship and the Sacrament of Baptism

The origin and meaning of the sacrament of baptism is less precise than the beginnings of the Lord's Supper. The Gospels contain no indication that Jesus instituted or practiced the rite of baptism. In the context of a report of a controversy between the disciples of John the Baptizer and the disciples of Jesus about who was baptizing more disciples, the Gospel of John inserts this parenthetical statement: "Although it was not Jesus himself but his disciples who baptized" (Jn. 4:1-2).

The synoptic gospels report John the Baptizer's baptism of Jesus, and the Gospel of John alludes to the event. The fact that Jesus sought baptism from John indicates that he regarded it as a meaningful experience in relation to the coming of the Kingdom of God. John the Baptizer is described as, "the voice of one crying out in the wilderness: 'Prepare the way of the Lord,'" (Mt. 3:3). The "way of the Lord" refers to the coming of the Messiah and the messianic kingdom. John said to all who would listen, "Repent, for the kingdom of heaven has come near" (Mt. 3:2). Both Mark and Luke say that John proclaimed "a baptism of repentance for the forgiveness of sins" (Mk. 1:4; Lu. 3:3).

John clearly announced the coming of the Messiah and of the messianic kingdom, but his call for his fellow Israelites to repent and be baptized did not fit the messianic expectation of the scribes and Pharisees. They knew baptism as a ritual administered to Gentiles who became Jewish proselytes. For this reason, they undoubtedly found John's message offensive. (See Lu. 3:7-8.) The thrust of John's teachings was that citizenship in the coming messianic kingdom would be determined, not by ethnic identity as a Jew and a satisfactory record of the observance of the law, but by a radical re-orientation of one's whole being. Baptism was a sign of this radical transformation.

In seeking baptism from John, Jesus indicated agreement with this understanding. In his own teachings Jesus incorporated this understanding of how one enters the Kingdom of God. Indeed, John anticipated this expansion of the meaning of baptism when he said of the coming Messiah, "He will baptize you with the Holy Spirit and fire" (Lu. 3:16).

Though there is no record in the Gospels that Jesus instituted the sacrament of baptism, in the manner of his institution of the Lord's Supper, Matthew 28:19 states that he commanded his disciples to practice the sacrament. In the explicit command to "make disciples of all nations, baptizing them in the name of the Father and of the Son and of the Holy Spirit," Jesus transformed this ritual as he had transformed the Passover. In connecting it explicitly with the proclamation of the Gospel, Jesus made baptism a sign of the covenant of grace.

The Confession of Faith says, "Baptism symbolizes the baptism of the Holy Spirit and is the external sign of the covenant which marks membership in the community of faith" (5.18). The Confession goes on to explain how this sign functions. "In this sacrament the church witnesses to God's initiative to claim persons in Christ, forgive their sins, grant them grace, shape and order their lives through the work of the Holy Spirit, and set them apart for service" (5.18). John the Baptizer alluded to this kind of transformation of meaning when he said that Jesus would baptize with the Holy Spirit and with fire.

Baptism is not something which persons do. It is not an act of obedience to God. It is something which God does. It is a gift of God through the ministry of the church. Baptism is a gift of God because it is a sign of God's covenant of grace. Understood in this sense, baptism is an evangelical proclamation. When performed as an act of public witness, it is a testimony of God's unmerited grace. As the Confession says, "In this sacrament the church witnesses to God's initiative to claim persons in Christ" (5.18). In this spirit, Martin Luther advised believers who became weak and fearful to remember their baptism.

As a sign of the covenant of grace, the Confession of Faith says that baptism "is administered to infants, one or both of whose parents or guardians affirm faith in Jesus Christ and *assume the responsibilities of the covenant*" (5.19, italics added). In this sense baptism also represents a transformation of the rite of circumcision. In the Old Testament, circumcision was a sign of the covenant. (See Gen. 17:9-14.) Paul understood the circumcision/baptism transformation when he wrote, "Circumcision is a matter of the heart. . . It is spiritual and not literal" (Rom. 2:29).

Colossians 2:11-12 also reflects this transformation when it calls baptism "a spiritual circumcision." Paul notes an important consequence of this transformation in Galatians 3:27-28. Male Jewish children and Gentile proselytes underwent circumcision. In contrast, Paul observed, "As many of you as were baptized in Christ have clothed yourselves in Christ. . . . There is no longer male and female; for all of you are in Christ."

The meaning of the baptism of infants is the same as that for adults. It is the sign of God's initiative to claim persons in Christ. For this reason, it is critical that at least one of the parents or guardians of the child affirm faith in Jesus Christ in order to insure that the parent(s) will teach the child the meaning of this sign of the covenant. When this is done, together with appropriate teachings concerning the meaning of the emerging inclination to sin, this sacrament may become a powerful, evangelical proclamation to the baptized child. When the child attains an appropriate level of understanding and responsibility, he or she may come to a personal confirmation of the baptism and a personal affirmation of faith in Jesus Christ as Savior.

The Confession of Faith goes on to say that baptism is a sign of the work of the Holy Spirit. Through the Holy Spirit God works to "forgive (persons) their sins, grant them grace, shape and order their lives" (5.18). This miracle of God's grace, to which baptism points, is what Jesus described as being born of the Spirit. It is through this birth from above that persons enter the Kingdom of God. In an apparent reference to baptism with water as a sign of baptism by the Holy Spirit, Jesus said, "Very truly I tell you, no one can enter the kingdom of God without being born of water and Spirit" (Jn. 3:5). It should come as no surprise, then, that the book of Acts usually associates the practice of baptism with the gift of the Holy Spirit. (See Acts 2:38; 9:17-19; 10:44-48; 19:1-7.)

Baptism with water as a sign of the baptism of the Holy Spirit is also a witness to salvation through the death and resurrection of Jesus Christ. In Romans 6:3-4, Paul wrote, "Do you not know that all of us who have been baptized into Christ Jesus were baptized into his death? Therefore we have been buried with him in baptism into death, so that just as Christ was raised from the dead by the glory of the Father, we too might walk in newness of life." One of the important insights of this text is its testimony to the death and resurrection of Christ Jesus as a single event of God's redemption. It is in the resurrection of Jesus Christ that the hope of newness of life lies. The death of Christ on the cross is a death to sin, but the resurrection of Christ is a resurrection to newness of life.

This passage also raises questions about the mode of baptism. Paul's language in Romans 6:1-11 may certainly reflect the practice of baptism by immersion. On the other hand, circumstances of the baptism of the Philippian jailer make that mode of immersion unlikely. (See Acts 16:29-34.) However, the New Testament contains no explicit discussion of the mode of baptism, nor does it use terms that must be translated pouring, sprinkling, or immersion.

Christian literature from as early as the 2nd century indicates that individuals and congregations used different modes, probably contingent on circumstances. The Confession of Faith says that "pouring or sprinkling of water . . . fittingly symbolizes the baptism of the Holy Spirit" (5.21). At the same time, the Confession recognizes the lack of a clear definition of mode in Scripture, and concludes, "The validity of the sacrament is not dependent on the mode of administration" (5.21).

Finally, the Confession of Faith says that in baptism the Holy Spirit sets persons apart for service. This refers to the calling, or full time vocation, of every Christian. Referring to ordained ministers and certain lay workers in the church as persons called to full-time Christian service is erroneous. The implication is that, at best, other Christians are engaged in part-time Christian service. This is contrary to both Scripture and the Confession of Faith. Every Christian's call is to full-time Christian service, and the gift of the Holy Spirit in baptism serves as ordination to this vocation.

For Discussion

1. How do you react to the claim that the first calling of the church is to the corporate worship of God? How does the worship practice of your particular congregation demonstrate your understanding of this claim?
2. How do you evaluate the worship of your church? Do you usually think of worship of God on the Lord's Day as a service directed to God, or as a service for the benefit of the people? Do people generally evaluate public worship in terms of how much they get out of it? What are they required to put into it?
3. How might the worship of your church on the Lord's day be different if those who plan and direct it viewed it more consciously as a celebration of the resurrection of Jesus Christ?
4. How do you react to the view of Luther and Calvin that corporate worship on the Lord's Day should always include the oral proclamation of the Word and its visible presentation in the Eucharist? How do you think your congregation might react to more frequent celebration of the Sacrament of the Lord's Supper?
5. What provisions exist in the educational ministry of your church both to teach baptized children the meaning of their baptism, and to assist parents in fulfilling their vows in this regard?

CHAPTER 11

THE CHURCH IN MISSION

Read Confession of Faith 5.10-5.11, 5.28-6.05; Constitution 1.1-2.1, 2.30, 2.51, 2.61-2.84, 3.02, 4.5, 5.6, 8.5, 9.4 and Scriptures listed for these sections.

Introduction

The Confession of Faith says, "The church in the world never exists for itself alone, but to glorify God and work for reconciliation through Christ" (5.09). The church serves God through worship and witness. In describing the content of worship, the Confession lists "praise, confession, thanksgiving, love and commitment to service" (5.13). The mission of the church is to serve. For this reason, many often call the church the servant community.

In baptism the Holy Spirit sets persons apart for service. The number of times the Confession refers to call to service is little short of remarkable. The Confession of Faith affirms that "God's will is sufficiently disclosed for persons to respond to it in worship, love *and service*" (1.09, italics added). Interpreting the meaning of the image of God in persons, the Confession says, "To reflect the divine image is to worship, love and *serve God*" (1.11, italics added).

Though God calls all persons to worship, love and service, this call is a special one for persons liberated from bondage to sin and death through the life, death and resurrection of Jesus Christ. Under the topic of "Providence," the Confession affirms that God guides the covenant community "in her mission of witness and service *in the world*" (1.17, italics added). The experience of sanctification, being set apart as servants in the world, is fundamental to what it means to be born of the Holy Spirit (COF 4.21). The worship of this community should always include a commitment to the service of God in the world. (See COF 5.14). Even the celebration of the Eucharist includes "a commitment to the *work and service of Christ's church*" (COF 5.25, italics added).

In all the references to a call to service, two things stand out. First, people serve God. In its most profound sense service is a response of gratitude and thanksgiving to God for the love, patience, forgiveness, and providence which members of the covenant community have received from God. This is the thrust of the parable recorded in Matthew 25. Those who inherited the Kingdom of God ministered to God in Christ when they visited persons in prison, cared for the sick, welcomed strangers, clothed the naked and gave food and drink to those who were hungry and thirsty.

The second thing to notice about the Confession's references to service is that it is service in the world. The church is not called to serve itself, but to serve people in the world. For this reason the church can more appropriately name many of its programs ministries, services to people. The criterion by which the church judges its faithfulness in its mission is both in what is going on at the church and what the church is doing in the world.

Church Government, Instrument of Service

The Confession of Faith says, "Jesus Christ as Lord and head of the church has entrusted the government of the church to officers who make decisions that will guide the life and *ministry* [service] of the covenant community" (5.32, italics added). The Cumberland Presbyterian Church has a "Constitution," "Rules of Discipline," and "Rules of Order," but the government of the church does not primarily consist of the enforcement of these documents. Rather, it is the use of these documents, and the organizational structures and procedures they outline, to do the mission of the church. Church government should be an instrument for service.

The Preamble to the Constitution says, "The purpose of church government is to aid the church in performing its mission" (COF p. 23). The officers who constitute the judicatories of the church–session, presbytery, synod, General Assembly–are said to have "the responsibility to serve the church," by making decisions that will "guide the life and *ministry*" of the church (COF 5.32, italics added). Persons who constitute these judicatories and their agencies should always focus on serving the church so that it may better serve in the world. A legalistic preoccupation with the documents of church government and a bureaucratic preoccupation with its organizational structures serve only to divert attention, energies and resources away from the performance of mission.

The Preamble to the Constitution says, "Although no detailed form of church government is laid down in scripture, the connectional nature of the church is clearly affirmed" (COF p. 23). Local congregations do not stand alone in performing their mission. They are connected to each other as a way of affirming the universal nature of the church. In this connection they give encouragement to each other and join with each other in the performance of those parts of the mission of the church which individual congregations cannot do alone. The Constitution states, "the

Presbyterian form embodies the *connectional nature of the church in a manner compatible with scripture*" (COF, p. 23, italics added).

As the basic unit of this representative form of government, the session is directly involved in aiding the performance of the mission of the church. In the broadest and most fundamental sense, the session is or should be a missionary society. The elders and pastor, who constitute the session, are responsible "to lead the members in all those *ministries* which belong to the church" (Const. 2.51, italics added). The work of the session is not confined to making decisions that will guide the life and ministry of the church. The pastor and elders who constitute the session are responsible to lead the congregation in the performance of this ministry.

In order for a congregation to be effective in service it must be in good spiritual condition. Such a condition will be reflected in the joyful, enthusiastic quality of its worship; an eagerness to study and understand the principle teachings of Scripture; a vibrant unity of spirit; a strong determination to witness to the Gospel; and a commitment to a ministry to people in need. The pastor and the elders who constitute the session bear the responsibility for exercising such pastoral care of the people necessary to enable the congregation to fulfill its mission. The Constitution is clear on this point: "The elders who comprise the session share with the minister in charge in the pastoral oversight of the particular church" (2.71; See also 4.5).

The first and most vital connectional link for the congregation is with the presbytery. This link exists through the pastor, through one or more elders whom the session elects as delegates to the meetings of presbytery, and through persons who serve on presbyterial boards and agencies. According to the Constitution, presbytery has pastoral oversight of ministers and congregations (5.6). This oversight includes an active concern for their spiritual health and for their commitment to the service of God in the larger arena of the presbyterial bounds.

The connectional ties that bind congregations together in a presbytery are extended through its representatives to the synod and General Assembly. In particular, the connectional tie through presbyterial representatives to the General Assembly binds all congregations together in ministry as the Cumberland Presbyterian Church. This connectional tie gives opportunity for a congregation to share in the mission of the church throughout the nation and around the world. The General Assembly "constitutes the bond of union, peace, correspondence and mutual confidence among all its churches and judicatories" (Const. 9.2).

To the degree that the connectional tie of a congregation to the General Assembly is real and meaningful, the congregation will begin to catch a glimpse of the "one, holy, universal apostolic church of Christ, who is her head and Lord" (COF 5.01). The letters of Paul in the New Testament clearly demonstrate the importance of this "bond of union, peace, correspondence and mutual confidence." Speaking of ministers and congregations which he and others had nurtured and developed, Paul said, "For we are God's servants, *working together*; you are God's field, God's building " (1 Cor. 3:9, italics added).

Through the connectional nature of the Presbyterian system of church government, representatives of the people, from the session of the local church to the General Assembly, make decisions and plans and lead the church in its mission. The mission to which God calls the church, and which its government should enable its members to perform, begins with the service of witness. The Confession says plainly that the church "is commissioned to witness to all persons who have not received Christ as Lord and Savior" (5.28). In becoming the persons God intends them to be, Christians bear witness to their Lord, and serve God and neighbors in the vocations of their common life (6.01).

Witnessing Through Oral Testimony

What it means to be a witness and to give testimony is an important issue for discipleship. One context for examining this idea is a court of law. An event has occurred; something has happened. Individuals give testimony about what they saw and heard; they relate the facts concerning the event. Persons take an oath before giving testimony, promising to tell the truth, and nothing but the truth, so help them God.

An analysis of this description shows these important components: First, an event occurs. Second, persons who see what happened come forward. Third, these persons swear to tell the truth about what happened, to give testimony about the event. This process parallels the Christian's call to give witness to the Gospel.

First, an event did occur, the Christ event–the birth, life, death and resurrection of Jesus called the Christ. Second, the followers of Jesus witnessed this event. Third, those witnesses gave testimony about this event which they have sworn, at the risk of their lives, to be true.

At this point, some differences between their testimony and testimony in a court of law begin to appear. Their testimony went beyond the facts concerning the event, beyond what any person could have observed, and affirmed that God was doing and saying something in the event. It was for this truth about the event that they were willing to risk their lives. In fact, some of the followers of Jesus faced death because they persisted in their claim that in and through the Christ event God was saying and doing things. Thus it was that the Greek word for witness, *martus*, acquired a new meaning and became the word we know as martyr.

Some may question how persons who did not see what happened, those who were not eyewitnesses to the Christ event, can in any sense be called witnesses. First, they can claim knowledge of the facts concerning this event on the basis of the written account of eyewitnesses, whose testimony concerning the basic facts has stood through the centuries. Second, they can affirm from their own experience the truth of what the eyewitnesses claimed God was saying and doing in the birth, life, death and resurrection of Jesus the Christ. They can also point to thousands of persons through the centuries who have risked their lives in order to give this testimony.

Several important things about these latter-day witnesses and about their testimony stand out. First, they need to get the facts straight by poring over the testimony of the first witnesses, recorded in the four Gospels. Attorneys working with persons preparing to give testimony in a court of law will rehearse with them, to insure that they won't become confused and stumble while giving testimony.

With respect to testimony about what the facts mean, latter-day witnesses must pore over the testimony of the original witnesses concerning what God was saying and doing in Jesus Christ, and reflect on this meaning in relation to their own experience. This involves identifying this testimony, as it appears interwoven with factual information about the Christ event in the Gospels. It also involves a careful examination of the testimony, recorded in the Book of Acts, of Peter, Paul and others who focused on the meaning of what had happened in the Christ event. This should be followed by careful and continuous study of the rest of the books of the New Testament, which are devoted entirely to the meaning of the Christ event–explanations of what God was doing and saying in Jesus the Christ.

Such study will make clear what the Confession of Faith means when it says, "The church, being nurtured and sustained by worship, by proclamation [hearing the story and meaning of the Gospel], and *study of the word*, and by celebration of the sacraments, is commissioned to witness to all persons who have not received Christ as Lord and Savior" (5.28, italics added). The Confession further identifies the content of the testimony expected, saying, "The covenant community is responsible to give witness to the mighty acts of God in the life, death, and resurrection of Jesus Christ" (5.31).

The opportunity, privilege and responsibility to witness to God's grace belongs to the whole church, not simply to ordained ministers. Every believer receives a commission to be a witness; the Holy Spirit anoints them for this service. The sacrament of baptism is the sign of this vocation. This sacrament is the church's witness to "God's initiative to claim persons in Christ, forgive their sins, grant them grace, shape and order their lives through the work of the Holy Spirit, and *set them apart for service"* —for the service of witness (5.18, italics added).

After stressing the importance and role of believers as witnesses to the Gospel, the Confession of Faith goes on to make two other important claims. First, while "respecting persons who adhere to other religions, Christians are responsible to share with them the good news of salvation through Jesus Christ" (5.30). A witness should not ridicule or run roughshod over persons with divergent religious beliefs. The witness should give testimony to the Gospel respectfully, in the spirit of love and humility.

The second point the Confession stresses is that, though critically important, the witness of believers does not limit God's communication of the Gospel to other people. "Where and when this witness [that of believers] is lacking, God is not without a witness" (5.31). This appears to be what Paul meant when he said, "When Gentiles, who do not possess the law, do instinctively what the law requires, these, though not having the law, are a law unto themselves. They show that what the law requires is written on their hearts, to which *their own conscience also bears witness . . ."* (Rom. 2:14-15, italics added).

The section of the Confession entitled "The Call and Work of the Holy Spirit" also supports this claim. While the "Holy Spirit works through the scripture, the sacraments, the corporate worship of the covenant community, *the witness of the believer in word and deed,"* it is not confined to these means (4.02, italics added). The Holy Spirit also works "in ways beyond human understanding," moving "on the hearts of sinners, convincing them of their sins and their need for salvation, and inclining them to repentance and faith toward God" (4.02).

Witnessing Through Lifestyle

Common wisdom indicates that actions speak louder than words. This is certainly the case with respect to the witness of Christians. Who they are and how they act, individually and as a community, constitute a powerful witness in the world. It is this witness that either establishes or compromises the credibility of all oral testimony. In a court of law, the bad, unreliable character of a person may undermine the credibility of his or her testimony as a witness. For Christians, the issue is not simply one of the lifestyle or character of an individual, but of the church as a community of people.

The covenant community is one of the dominant concepts in both the Old and New Testaments. God has not and does not simply call individuals out of the world; God calls a community to be God's people. God calls this community to be different from the rest of the world's people. God calls them to be holy, set apart for a particular purpose. God also calls them to practice a particular lifestyle. (See Ex. 19:6; 1 Pet. 2:9-10.)

Another way to describe this peculiar community of people is to say that they are citizens of the Kingdom of God, ruled by Jesus the Messiah (Christ). Their citizenship in the Kingdom of God determines their lifestyle. This lifestyle sets them apart from the rest of the world, which does not acknowledges Jesus Christ as Lord or Ruler. Their witness in the world is not simply that of a group of separate individuals, but of a community.

The Confession of Faith describes the church in this way: It is a community of people who "are united to Christ by faith" and "to one another in love." In this community they "share the grace of Christ with one another," and "bear one another's burdens." As a community of this kind of people, they then "reach out to all other persons" (5.10).

The special bond that holds this community together is God's covenant of grace. The community of faith is made up of people who have been set free from bondage to sin and death, free to love God and each other, and free to serve God and the people of the world. The Confession of Faith puts it this way: "This freedom, rooted in love, not fear, enables persons to become who God intends them to be, to bear witness to their Lord, and to serve God and neighbors in the vocations of their common life" (6.01).

Christian freedom, the defining characteristic of the Christian lifestyle, is radical in nature and very different from ordinary human freedom. Ordinary human freedom can be defined as freedom of choice, the freedom of the will. By contrast, Christian freedom is the freedom to love, the freedom to love God and persons. The freedom to love is the freedom to give one's self to the service of God and persons.

Paul, more than any other New Testament writer, understood the radical lifestyle to which Jesus called his followers. To the Galatians he wrote, "For freedom Christ has set us free. Stand firm, therefore and do not submit again to the yoke of slavery" (Gal. 5:1). Paul defined this yoke of slavery as a continuing bondage to sin and the law. The Confession of Faith defines freedom from the bondage of sin as freedom "from the shackles, oppression, and shame of sin and sinful forces" (6.01). It is freedom from what the Confession earlier describes as being "inclined to sin in all aspects of (one's) being" (2.03). It is freedom from radical self-centeredness.

According to Paul, freedom from the law meant freedom from the delusion that one can earn and/or keep one's salvation by obeying a set of rules. Paul labeled legalistic religion as a curse, and said that "Christ redeemed us from the curse of the law." (See Gal. 3:1-19.) The curse of the law is twofold. On one hand, it feeds self-centeredness to produce self-righteousness. On the other hand, it creates fear because of the awareness that no one can obey the law perfectly.

In letters to churches, Paul never tired of the effort to define both the nature of Christian freedom and the lifestyle which believers are set free to practice. In a long passage in the Roman letter, Paul insisted, "Owe no one anything, except to love one another; for one who has loved another has fulfilled the law." (See Rom. 12:1-20; 13:8-10; Gal. 5:13-15, 22-26; 1 Cor. 13:1-13; see also 1 Jn. 4:7-21.)

In the Philippian letter, Paul defined this lifestyle as having the mind of Christ. By this he meant doing "nothing from selfish ambition or conceit, but in humility (regarding) others as better than yourselves." (See Phil. 2:1-11). This is exactly what Jesus the Christ did, when he "emptied himself, taking the form of a slave, . . . (and) humbled himself and become obedient to the point of death–even death on a cross" (Phil. 2:7-8).

When the world looks at a church which demonstrates the mind of Christ, it will be struck by the radical nature of its lifestyle. Paul speaks of the utter importance of such a lifestyle in his letter to the Corinthians. When he encountered jealousy and quarreling in the church, he asked, "Who sees anything different in you?"

At the same time, being part of such a community makes possible the practice of the radical lifestyle that Jesus laid out in Matthew 5:1–7:14. The strenuous, demanding nature of this radical lifestyle is such that a lone individual will be hard put to remain faithful. Perhaps that is the reason that Jesus observed that this lifestyle is indeed narrow, and that few find it. Christians need the strength God gives them through the worship and fellowship of the covenant community. God calls Christians to practice this lifestyle, not separated from the world, but "in the vocations of their common life" (COF 6.01).

History has demonstrated time and time again that when the church practices this lifestyle in the world it encounters persecution. This lifestyle is a threat to the ways of the world. The governments of the world have characteristically been very uneasy in dealing with communities of people whose freedom is rooted in love, not fear, people who yield ultimate allegiance to Jesus Christ as Lord. This is so because these people have dared, "in Christian conscience (to) oppose any form of injustice." (See COF 6.01, 6.05.) For this reason, faithful witnesses, both in oral testimony and in the testimony of lifestyle, have faced the possibility of martyrdom.

Paul wrote to the church at Philippi, "Make my joy complete; be of the *same mind,* having the same love. . . . Do nothing from selfish ambition or conceit, but in humility regard others as better than yourselves. Let each of you look not to your own interests, but to the interests of others" (Phil. 2:2-4, italics added). Having the same mind is having the mind of Christ, "who though he was in the form of God, did not regard equality with God, as something to be exploited, but emptied himself, taking the form of a servant . . ." (Phil. 2:2-4).

For Discussion

1. It does matter what we call things. How would the work of your church be affected if you thought in terms of ministries instead of programs? How might participants react to changing from serving on committees to participating in ministries?
2. What is the significance of the connectional nature of the church in its performance of ministry? How does your presbytery, synod and the General Assembly aid your congregation in its ministry? How do they hinder it?
3. How confident are you with your ability to give testimony of the Christ event and its significance in your life? How might you respond to an unbeliever's questions about the role of faith in your life?
4. React to the claim that full-time Christian service applies to all believers and not only to clergy and other church professionals.
5. What evidence does your congregation and/or its members show of being set apart from the world? What is distinctive about the lifestyle of people with whom you share life and work in the church?
6. Discuss your understanding of Christian freedom. From what are we set free? What does our freedom enable us to do? How does Christian freedom differ from human freedom? What do you believe about freedom of the will?
7. What are some issues in your community and in the world to which your church needs to respond if it understands itself to be set apart from the world for service?

CHAPTER 12

THE CHURCH IN THE WORLD

Read Confession of Faith 6.06-6.22, 6.25-6.32 and Scriptures listed for these sections.

Introduction

In his prayer for his disciples, Jesus asked God not "to take them out of the world," but "to protect them from the evil one." He went on to say, "As you have sent me into the world, so I have sent them into the world." (See Jn. 17:1-19.) An important part of Christian life is involved in giving witness in the world by both speech and lifestyle. Christians give witness in the world "in the vocations of their common life" through "deeds of service and mercy exemplified by Christ, but also those ethical and moral choices that reflect Christian values and principles in all of life's relationships" (COF 6.01, 6.09).

When coupled with oral testimony to the Gospel and a lifestyle characterized by the freedom to love and serve others, this kind of ministry in the world is a powerful witness. Through "deeds of service and mercy," and through "ethical and moral choices that reflect Christian values and principles," the people of the covenant community give testimony to Jesus the Messiah, the Servant Lord. As the Confession says, the constant awareness of Christians that they are sinners saved by grace, "produces [in them] the desire to do good works" (COF 6.06). Ethical and moral choices that reflect Christian values and principles" are a response to God's grace.

Witness in Good Works

The Confession of Faith identifies good works as "deeds of service and mercy exemplified by Christ" (6.07). A deed of service is a deed performed to meet a need of one or more persons. A deed of mercy is an action performed to or for persons in dire straits, perhaps those suffering from neglect or discrimination in society. Elsewhere the Confession identifies such persons as "the poor, the oppressed, the sick, the helpless, . . . all victims of violence, and all those whom the law or society treats as less than persons for whom Christ died" (6.31).

The Confession goes on to say that Jesus sought out such persons.

The Confession calls the covenant community, which affirms the lordship of Christ, to follow him in this ministry. In a sweeping declaration, the Confession says, "The church has responsibility to minister to the needs of persons in every crisis, including physical and emotional illness, economic distress, natural disasters, accidents due to carelessness, and death" (6.22). In the scriptural record of Christ's ministry, the church finds an understanding of the motive, nature, and approach of such good works.

Wherever Jesus went, teaching and proclaiming the good news of the kingdom, a crowd of people followed him. They brought to him "the lame, the blind, the mute and many others"(Mt. 15:30). On one occasion, "When he saw the crowd, he had compassion on them, because they were harassed and helpless, like sheep without a shepherd" (Mt. 9:36). Repeatedly, to the horror of the scribes and Pharisees, and sometimes the dismay of his own disciples, Jesus gave particular attention to the outcasts of society. Lepers, prostitutes, tax collectors and others excluded from normal social relations found a friend in Jesus.

In one of his parables Jesus said, "When you give a luncheon or a dinner, do not invite your friends or your brothers or your relatives or rich neighbors, . . . But when you give a banquet, invite the poor, the crippled, the lame and the blind" (Lu. 14:12-13). The writer of James focuses on this aspect of the ministry of Jesus. He argues that persons claiming to be Christian who show favoritism toward the rich while ignoring the poor have a dead faith. In a rhetorical question, he asks, "Has not God chosen the poor in the world to be rich in faith and to be heirs of the kingdom that he has promised to those who love him?" (Jas. 2:5).

If the church performs its ministry of service and mercy in the way which Christ exemplified" it will require a quality of spiritual life often not present in the simple performance of good deeds. The church will engage in ministry without fanfare or ulterior motives. As Jesus put it, "Whenever you give alms, do not sound a trumpet before you" (Mt. 6:2). Nor should the church see such a ministry as an enticement for potential church members.

Ministry springs from genuine compassion, in which the persons served do not feel robbed of their self-respect. The persons to whom Jesus ministered felt his unconditional acceptance of them as persons. Even when society labelled them unclean, Jesus did not hesitate to touch them. The ministry of Jesus was not discriminatory, directed only to the most promising prospects. He did not condition the healing of lepers on whether they showed appropriate gratitude for the benefit they received.

The ministry of the church is a redemptive ministry, one that costs the giver. The ministry of Jesus was redemptive in the fullest sense of the term, not simply a temporary Christmas basket or other gift. His immediate cost came in the form of opposition from the respectable people of society who tagged him as a person who spent his time with the no-good trash of the community. The rich and the powerful regarded his attempt to give hope to the hopeless, to be a voice for the poor and out-casts of society, as dangerous. The authorities charged him with being a revolutionary and took his life.

A Witness for Justice

The Confession of Faith identifies good works not only as "deeds of service and mercy," but also as "ethical and moral choices that reflect Christian values and principles in all of life's relationships" (6.09). The principle of justice is an important consideration among "Christian values and principles." Being a voice for justice is part of what it means to be a witness to the Gospel. The Confession puts it this way: "Such advocacy [i.e., for persons treated unjustly] involves not only opposition to all unjust laws and forms of injustice but even more support for those attitudes and actions which embody the way of Christ, which is to overcome evil with good" (6.31).

In an even more direct way, the Confession says, "The covenant community, governed by the Lord Christ, opposes, resists and seeks to change all circumstances of oppression–political, economic, cultural, racial--by which persons are denied the essential dignity God intends for them in the work of creation" (6.30). The church performs this ministry of "reconciliation, love, and justice among all persons, classes, races, and nations" (6.32).

The church, corporately and individually, speaks its message concerning issues of justice to civil governments. The Old Testament prophets serve as the biblical basis for such a witness. From Moses to Jeremiah, the great prophets called on governments to practice justice toward all people. They spoke for a God who is particularly concerned about the way the rich and powerful use governments to oppress the poor and defenseless.

Beginning with Moses, God shows a desire for compassionate justice. The poor and the resident alien were usually the first objects of injustice. Through Moses, God promised to hear the cries of those treated unjustly: "I will listen, for I am compassionate" (See Ex. 22:21-27; Lev. 19:33-37.) Amos was critical of dishonest practices in business and favoritism by judges, charging that the poor failed to get justice in the courts.

As objects of economic injustice, the poor often endured slavery to pay their debts. (See Amos 5:10-11; 8:4-6.) The prophets called on the government to "establish justice in the gate [courts]," and urged, "let justice roll down like waters, and righteousness like an everflowing stream" (5:15, 24).

Speaking directly to the leaders of government, Isaiah said, "The Lord enters into judgment with the elders and princes of his people. It is you who have devoured the vineyards. The spoil of the poor is in your houses" (Isa. 3:14). Micah was equally direct in his protest against injustices of government officials. "Their hands are skilled to do evil; the official and the judge ask for a bribe, and the powerful dictate what they desire; thus they pervert justice" (Mic. 7:3).

For the most part, the teachings of Jesus concerning justice appear within the context of the requirements for citizenship in the Kingdom of God. At the same time, however, he directed these teachings at the practices of the society of Palestine. Like the prophets, Jesus showed a passionate concern about the poor and the outcasts, but unlike the prophets Jesus did not address his message to the political rulers of Palestine. Some interpreters of the teachings of Jesus understand his example as a directive that the church should not get involved in political affairs.

Before drawing such conclusions, however, Christians should consider the differences between the political situations in Palestine at the time of the prophets and of Jesus and the contemporary setting. Palestine was an independent national state during the time of the prophets with a monarchy as the form of government. The prophet Samuel established the monarchy when he anointed Saul as the first king. Israel existed as a nation under God, in which both the people and the king pledged to do the will of God. (See 1 Sam. 12:6-18.) In this context, the prophets, who were citizens of the nation as well as spokespersons for God, called the government to give account before God of its actions.

Palestine was a colonial possession of the government of Rome when Jesus lived there. Most of the Jews in Palestine were not citizens of the Roman government and had no sense of ownership in this government. Rome treated criticisms of the civil government as dangerous signs of revolutionary attitudes and potential revolutionary actions. The Roman government ruthlessly suppressed persons making such criticisms. The Hebrew leaders of the Temple convinced the Roman authorities to bring such charges against Jesus, providing the official basis for his execution by the Roman governor.

At the same time, Rome worked out a deal with Jewish leaders in Palestine to grant the Jewish Sanhedrin the power and authority to govern the Jews in most areas of their lives. As long as the Jews paid their taxes to Rome, and did not engage in revolutionary rhetoric or activities, the Roman governor did not deal directly with the Jewish people. Such injustices as existed among the Jews became the responsibility of the Sanhedrin, a quasi-religious body.

In this context, Jesus often directed his teachings at the injustices which the Jewish leaders practiced or tolerated. Prohibitions against healing a person on the Sabbath is a case in point. (See Mk. 3:1-6). On another occasion Jesus criticized an elaborate legal loophole that permitted persons to avoid the responsibility for caring for their aged parents. (See Mk. 7:1-13.) In general, the treatment which the working poor received from their Jewish government was one of the reasons that they responded so favorably to the things he taught. On one occasion, when Jesus addressed Jewish leaders in the Temple, he charged that they "devoured widows' houses" (Mk. 12:35-40).

On another occasion Jesus described the common people as "harassed and helpless, like sheep without a shepherd" (Mt. 9:36). Clearly he felt that the Jewish leadership had failed them. The judgment of God which he pronounced against these leaders was as severe as any words of judgment the great prophets had spoken against the kings of their day. In his famous temple sermon, Jeremiah had charged that the leaders of Israel had oppressed "the alien, the orphan, and the widow;" he said that God's judgment would include the destruction of the temple. (See Jer. 7:1-20.) After having charged the leaders of the Israel of his day with devouring widows' houses, Jesus said that the temple would be destroyed. (See Mk. 13:1-2.)

Both the words of the prophets and the teachings and actions of Jesus make clear that God will hold a government accountable for the way it treats its people, especially the "poor, the oppressed, the sick, the helpless, . . . all victims of violence and all those whom the law or society treats as less than persons for whom Christ died" (COF 6.31). This accountability is a particular issue for a government established, as the prophet Samuel had said, under God.

The Confession does not confine the responsibility of the church toward government to that of a voice against injustice. It commits the church, and its individual members, to work for the enactment and administration of just laws. After asserting that "the purpose of civil government is to enable God's creation to live under the principles of justice and order," the Confession of Faith goes on to say: "It is the duty of people to participate in government, . . . especially in exercising the right to vote" (COF 6.28). The Confession continues: "It is the duty of Christians to enter civil offices . . . for the purpose of working for justice, peace, and the common welfare" (COF 6.28).

Witness Through Stewardship

The Confession of Faith says that God's purpose for civil government is that the whole creation, not simply the human community, shall "live under the principles of justice and order" (COF 6.27). This points to the basic meaning of the stewardship responsibility God gave persons for the whole creation. "So God created human kind in his image, . . . male and female he created them. God blessed them, and God said to them, 'Be fruitful and multiply, and fill the earth and *subdue it; and have dominion over (it)*'" (Gen. 1:27-30, italics added). The second account of creation in Genesis 2 completes the description of the stewardship responsibility which God gave persons. Not only did God give them authority and power over the creation, but God also made them responsible to care for it. (See Gen. 2:15.)

Tragically, the human family has rebelled against God, and one of the consequences of this rebellion has been a neglect and abuse of its stewardship responsibility for the creation. As Genesis 3:8-19 puts it, the ground was cursed because of the sin of the creatures made in the Divine image. The apostle Paul referred to this curse, saying that "the creation was subjected to futility; . . . [and] bondage to decay," and is "groaning" to be set free. (See Rom. 8:19-23.)

The Confession describes the impact of human sin on the creation in this way: "The alienation of persons from God affects the rest of creation, so that the whole creation stands in need of God's redemption" (2.06). In recent years the magnitude of the ecological crisis has revealed some of the effects of the neglect and abuse by persons of their stewardship responsibility to care for the whole creation.

The redemption of persons through Jesus Christ includes the redemption of their stewardship responsibility. This means, as the Confession says, that "the motive for Christian stewardship is gratitude for God's abundant love and mercy, accompanied by the desire to share all of God's gifts with others" (6.11). It follows then, that "all believers are responsible to God and to the covenant community for their stewardship" (6.14). This responsibility to God involves the care of the whole creation. The responsibility to the covenant community involves the uses of God's gifts in the ministry of the church.

A profound sense of awe at the beauty, order, vitality, majesty and goodness of the heavens and the earth, and of all living things is fundamental to the stewardship of caring for the creation. A deep sense of humility regarding the authority, power and responsibility to the care of the whole creation should accompany this profound sense of awe.

What happens to the balance of nature as a consequence of human activity is a matter of Christian concern. The human family has abused its power and authority over the creation and has begun to trash the planet earth, and is beginning to extend that abuse into the heavens. The scientific community is sounding alarms about the magnitude of this abuse, but scientists often express this concern in terms of human survival. The motive of Christian stewardship is not human survival, but thanksgiving to God for all the glory, power, wisdom, beauty, goodness and love disclosed in the creation.

What happens to all living things as a consequence of human activity is a matter of Christian concern. All plants and animals are sacred, because they were created by God for a purpose. The second account of creation in Genesis 2 emphasizes the stewardship responsibility of persons to care for living things in two ways. First, the human family was "put in the garden of Eden to till and keep it" (Gen. 2:15). The world is a magnificent garden of trees, flowers, herbs, vegetables, grasses, and all manner of plants; and God made persons the gardeners. What an awesome responsibility.

Second, God established a special relationship in creation between persons and all the animals, and this accentuated the stewardship responsibility which persons have for them. God created the animals as helpers and partners for persons, gave persons the privilege of naming them. Both the way animals help persons and the devotion they give to persons reflects this special relationship. Saint Francis of Assisi understood the profound depth of this relationship, so he referred to the animals as his brothers and sisters. The abuse and exploitation of animals by persons, deliberately or by neglect, must grieve the heart of God. Indeed, it was Jesus the Christ who said that not even a sparrow falls to the ground without the Father's will. (See Mt. 10:29.) Beyond caring for the creatures, the Confession says, "Christian stewardship acknowledges that all of life and creation is a trust from God, *to be used for God's glory and service*. . . . These gifts are to be shared with all, especially the poor" (COF 6.10, italics added).

In Corinthians 12:7, Paul wrote, "To each is given the manifestation of the Spirit for the common good." Though he was talking about the use of personal gifts within the life of the church, the text has a broader meaning. By their nature as new creatures in Christ Jesus, Christians are responsible to God for all they are, including their gifts. This is by virtue of both their original creation and their new creation by the Holy Spirit.

Early in the first Corinthian letter, speaking about the misuse and abuse of human sexuality, Paul wrote: "Do you not know that your body is a temple of the Holy Spirit within you, which you have from God, and that you are not your own? For you were bought with a price. Therefore glorify God in your body" (6:19-20). Whether it is the gift of human sexuality, gifts to use in gainful employment, gifts for the performing arts, or gifts of any other sort, Christians are responsible to use God's gifts for the common good.

The most fundamental act of Christian stewardship is giving one's self to God. Commenting on the generosity of the Christians in Macedonia in their contributions to a fund for the saints in Jerusalem, Paul said, "They gave themselves first to the Lord" (2 Cor. 8:5). This response of thanksgiving to God is the necessary framework in which Christians make decisions about the use and distribution of all things which God has given to the human family for its welfare.

The first explicit teachings in Scripture about the use of things are found in the books of the Law. These teachings assume that land is the basic source for all things necessary for human welfare. Accordingly, God said to the people of Israel, "The land shall not be sold into perpetuity, for the land is mine; with me you are but aliens and tenants" (Lev. 25:23). As a means of preventing the concentration of land ownership in the hands of a few people, and of emphasizing that the land belongs to God, the Torah provided for a Year of Jubilee, when all debts were cancelled and all land was returned to its original owners.

However quaint and impossible these concepts and practices may seem today, they point to the claim made by the Confession of Faith: "*The natural world is God's.* Its resources, beauty, and order *are given in trust to all people,* to conserve, enjoy, *to use for the welfare of all,* and thereby to glorify God" (COF 1.12, italics added). In terms of Christian stewardship, this means that Christians should insist in both word and deed that "these gifts of God are to be shared with all, especially the poor" (COF 6.10).

The commonly accepted understanding of stewardship as giving through the church takes on new meaning when understood in the broad concept of Christian stewardship as caring for the whole creation. The Confession of Faith includes five sections under the heading "Christian Stewardship," only one of which deals with "giving through the church." (See 6.13). This understanding does not minimize the importance of Christian stewardship. It emphasizes that giving through the church is only one way to witness to God's grace through Christian stewardship.

The biblical basis for giving in and through the church begins with a number of Old Testament texts, principally in the Torah (Law). (See Gen. 14:17-20; 28:10-22; Lev. 27:30-33; Num. 18:21-32; Deut. 14:22-29; 26:1-13; Neh. 10:35-39; 12:44-47; Mal. 3:8-12). The teachings in these texts concerning offerings made to God in and through the church include: (1) These offerings are fundamentally acts of the worship of God, in which the motives of gratitude and thanksgiving predominate. (2) One use of offerings, notably the tithe, is for the maintenance of the places of worship and the provision of a livelihood for priests and others who care for the places of worship and lead the people in worship. (3) A further use of the tithe is in the care of the poor.

The Law instructed the Israelites to give the Lord a tithe (one tenth) of their herds, flocks, grain, fruits, oil--all the produce from the land. Giving the tithe was a response of gratitude and thanksgiving for the produce from the land, and for the redemption of Israel from bondage in Egypt. However, as Scripture makes clear, sin allows the selfish interests of persons to influenced their motives. Jacob attempted to bargain with God over the tithe (Gen. 28:22). As an incentive to persons to be more faithful in giving their tithes, the prophet Malachi promised that God would reward tithers with material prosperity (Mal. 3:8-12).

These two examples, however, are exceptions to the fundamental emphasis on giving out of gratitude and thanksgiving to God. The Old Testament is consistent in its identification of two basic uses for the tithe. The community of faith used it to construct, maintain and operate places of worship; and for the livelihood of priests and others who cared for the places of worship and led the people in worship. They also distributed offerings to help the poor, the alien, and others who had limited means of economic support. The tithe was only one of many offerings which the Israelites gave to God in and through the church.

The New Testament indicates that giving the tithe and other offerings to God in and through the church had become part of a legalistic religion. The motives in this religion with respect to the tithe were akin to those of Jacob and of the text from Malachi: tithing was as an act of obedience to the law, for which rewards would follow, both in this life and the life to come. The three references to tithing in the Gospels appear in the context of Jesus' devastating critique of the legalistic religion of the scribes and Pharisees. (See Mt. 23:23-24; Lu. 11:42-44; 18:9-14.)

The religion of works of the scribes and Pharisees probably dated back to the time of Ezra. It assumed that the basic relationship between God and the human family is a covenant of law, as represented by persons before a judge. Obedience to the law brought salvation, acceptance by God and the covenant community, and other rewards such as good health and material prosperity. By contrast, Jesus taught that the human family relates to God personally in a covenant of grace, as children relate to a parent. (See Lu. 15:11-31.) Jesus reclaimed gratitude and thanksgiving as motives for giving and stressed that giving should be done sacrificially. This was the point of the stories of the rich young ruler and the poor widow in Luke 18:18-25 and 21:1-4.

The writings of Paul interpret Jesus' teachings and actions concerning giving most clearly. Paul never referred to the tithe, but he did talk about regular and proportionate giving. Members of the community of faith were to bring gifts on the Lord's Day in proportion to the way they had prospered. (See 1 Cor. 16:1-2.) Paul did not elaborate on what he meant by proportionate. He did, however, observe that the giving of the people in the churches in Macedonia had been "beyond their means," and he explained this sacrificial giving by saying that "they gave themselves first to the Lord." (See 2 Cor. 8:1-5.)

This profound sense of gratitude and thanksgiving for the grace of God shown in Jesus Christ leads to grace giving. It is the adventure of grace giving that the Confession of Faith has in mind where it says, "Tithing as a scriptural guide for giving, is an adventure of faith" (6.13). Persons who give graciously and begin at the level of a tithe, will experience more exciting adventures in giving beyond their means. As Paul noted about the Macedonians, the possibility of this occurring will be related to the degree to which persons "give themselves first to the Lord."

Witness Through Family Life

The Confession of Faith says, "God created the family as the primary community in which persons experience love, companionship, support, protection, discipline, encouragement, and other blessings" (6.15). This means that the family is of fundamental importance in forming persons as witnesses to God in their decisions and deeds. When families are as God created them to be, the church simply builds upon and extends the scope of the witness of their members.

Tragically, this basic community was and continues to be the first victim of the sin and rebellion of persons against God. The fundamental impact of original sin on the family changed its nature. God created the family to be a community in which relationships are characterized by self-giving love, *agape*. Because of sin, the family became a community in which relationships are characterized by self-getting love, *eros*.

The relationship of the man and woman in marriage demonstrates this corruption of relationships in the family. In the Genesis account, after their sin and rebellion against God, the man and woman tried to cover up their nakedness. Because of sin they felt guilty and were uncomfortable not only in the presence of God but of each other. This alienation from God and from each other corrupted all aspects of the family.

Among other consequences of sin, God's gift of human sexuality, a sign of that mystery of grace when two persons become one, becomes corrupt, an occasion for conflict and violence. In a further indication of the perversion of what God intended to be a partnership, the Genesis account says a woman's "desire shall be for (her) husband, and he shall rule over (her)" (Gen. 3:16). God's continuing creation of persons as a result of sexual relations between men and women, intended as a source of joy, became a source of pain and sorrow. The gift of work, by which the needs of the family were to be met, became a source of frustration and a burden. (See Gen. 3:17-19.)

The redemption of men and women includes the redemption of their family relationships. In its redeemed state, the marriage relationship may be a symbol of the relationship of Christ and the church. (See Eph. 5:11-33.) However, this understanding requires a new interpretation of what it means to be head, and to rule over. Jesus both taught and demonstrated that being head and ruling over means to be a servant, even to the point of giving your life for persons. (See Phil. 2:5-8.) Only in this radical sense can the marriage relationship serve as an analogy for the relationship of Christ and the church.

The critical role of the family as "the primary community in which persons experience love, companionship, support, protection, discipline, encouragement, and other blessings" (COF 6.15), explains the deep concern in the Confession of Faith for its redemption. The first step in this redemption is the effort of the church to interpret the true nature of marriage which the Confession calls "a covenant relationship under God," and a "lifetime commitment" (6.18). Families built on such an understanding of the marriage relationship are a powerful witness in the world, where self-getting is the standard pattern of human existence.

The Confession goes on to say that the church bears the responsibility to communicate its understanding of the marriage relationship by helping "persons prepare for marriage, for parental responsibilities, and for family life under God" (6.21). "When human weakness and sin threaten the marriage relationship, the covenant community has responsibility to uphold the sanctity of marriage and to help partners strengthen their relationship" (6.20).

Finally, because of the utter importance of the family as the primary community for the welfare of both parents and children, and recognizing the disastrous effects of broken families on the lives of their members, the church commits itself to a continuing ministry to the victims of divorce (COF 6.20). As the family of God, the church is responsible to reach out in caring love and helpfulness to persons whose lives have been shattered by the destruction of their primary community. In effect, the church family may become a surrogate family for those whose primary families have been disrupted if not destroyed. This is an important part of the witness of Christians through family life.

The church in the world, a community of people bound to God by the covenant of grace, lives under the rule of Jesus the Messiah. As the church worships, witnesses, and ministers in the world, it looks for the consummation of the Kingdom of God at the end of the age.

For Discussion

1. What are the basic characteristics of "deeds of service and mercy" as Jesus taught and exemplified them?
2. What are some of the ways in which your church and its individual members serve as a witness for justice? In what kinds of ministries might your church become involved if justice issues received more attention?
3. What are your reactions to the biblical bases for a ministry in the area of justice presented in this chapter?
4. What do the creation accounts teach about the stewardship responsibility of persons toward the world?
5. What are some responsible options for Christian involvement in the political system?
6. What evidence have you seen of the impact of sin on individual human families?

CHAPTER 13

THE CONSUMMATION OF ALL THINGS

Read Confession of Faith 7.01-7.08 and Scriptures listed for these sections.

Introduction

The Introduction to the 1984 Confession of Faith states that "the organizing principle of this confession is to tell the story the Bible tells in the way the Bible tells it" (p. xv). The story of the Bible begins in Genesis with God's creation of the heavens and the earth and ends in Revelation with God's creation of a new heaven and a new earth. Between the beginning and the end is the story of the rebellion of persons against God and the subsequent bondage of the whole creation to sin and death. An account of God's judgment and redemption of the world overlays this story of sin and death. As the Confession puts it, "In and through the scriptures, God speaks about creation, sin, judgment and salvation . . ." (1.05).

The end of the biblical story deals with the final act of God's judgment and redemption of the whole creation. The community of faith has used various terms to refer to this event–the end of the age, the second coming of Christ, the end of time, the consummation of the Kingdom of God. The Confession of Faith says that in this event "God consummates all life and history" (7.00). The key word is consummates. The world does not just come to an end. A consummation, an end that represents a completion of what God had undertaken, occurs. What will be brought to completion is all life and history, the whole creation.

Through the centuries the end of time, or the second coming of Christ, has been the subject of much speculation. People have asked questions regarding exactly what will happen, and when these things will come to pass. The 1814, 1883 and 1984 Cumberland Presbyterian Confessions of Faith all contain sections dealing with the end of time. The language of each Confession is restrained, and devoid of speculation about the details of when and how this event will occur.

Following the lead of all these Confessions, this commentary will focus on the meaning of the event, not on the details of when and how it will occur. Preoccupation with times and seasons, and the failure to distinguish between the reality of the event and the language used to describe it has obscured the meaning of what God will be doing in the event. Finite persons have as much difficulty comprehending exactly how time will end as they have understanding how time began. Both events are on the border between time and eternity, and are not easy to grasp. Finite persons must, then, be modest and humble as they confront these divine mysteries.

The Purpose of Life and History

Discussion of the purpose of all creation requires a focus on the will of God. What is God's will for the creation? What purpose of God does creation manifest? The Confession of Faith says, "God's will for people and all creation is altogether wise and good" and that "God's will is sufficiently disclosed for persons to respond to it in worship, love and service, yet they should hold in reverence the mystery and wonder of divine ways" (1.08). The Confession goes on to say, "Although revealed in scriptures and in the events of nature and history, God's will is made known supremely in the person of Jesus Christ, who did God's will even to death" (1.08, 1.09).

These sections of the Confession make several important affirmations. First, persons are able to know and understand some things about the will and purpose of God, but they should ever be mindful of the mystery of divine ways. Persons who claim to understand the exact scenario for the end of time should "hold in reverence and wonder the mystery of divine ways" (COF 1.09).

Second, the scripture reveals what persons can know about God's will and purpose in the events of nature and history. This revelation appears "supremely in the person of Jesus Christ" (COF 1.08). Such knowledge will show that "God's will for people and all creation is altogether wise and good" (COF 1.08) and that God is active in nature and history to accomplish the divine will. Finally, the will of God for the whole creation is that it manifest or disclose "God's glory, power, wisdom, beauty, goodness and love" (COF 1.10). In Scripture, the glory of God is synonymous with the presence of God. The purpose of all creation is to manifest the presence of God. The psalmist said that the heavens and the earth reveal the presence/glory of God (Ps. 19). Moses told the Israelites that when persons gather to worship God, the presence/glory of God is among them (Lev. 9:5-6, 23). Indeed, when persons fulfill their stewardship responsibility toward the world, they reflect the glory/presence of God, in whose image God created them (COF 6.10).

Because of the glory/presence of God in all creation, and particularly the personal presence of God with persons, the appropriate response of persons is to praise God–to give glory to God. It is no accident that the psalmists, who were very sensitive to God's presence in all creation, were continually giving glory / praise to God. Nor is it accidental that the two ancient ascriptions in Christian liturgy are the Doxology (Praise God) and the *Gloria Patri* (Glory Be to the Father). If the Confession's claim that the will / purpose of God "is made known supremely in the person of Jesus Christ" is true, then Christ manifests the full glory of God. This is exactly the claim of John 1:14: "The Word [who was God] became flesh and lived among us, and we have seen his glory . . ."

The presence / glory of God in the world, and particularly with the human family, is the presence of a God of power, wisdom, beauty, goodness, and love. It is, in fact, as 1 John 4:16 says, the presence of God who is love. A compelling evidence of God's presence in the creation as love appears in what the Confession calls God's "providential care over all creatures, people, nations and things" (1.13). The psalmist is most eloquent in praise of God's loving care of all creation. After recounting all the evidence of God's providence for the creation, the psalmist shouted, "I will sing to the Lord as long as I live; I will sing praises to my God while I have being" (Ps. 104:33).

As in the glory / presence of God, so also in the love of God. The full manifestation of God's love was and is in Jesus the Christ. As John 3:16 affirms, Jesus the Christ embodied the love of God. Jesus stated this understanding in such teachings as his statement that even sparrows and lilies of the field are under the loving care of God. He showed compassion toward all kinds of people, women and men from all walks of life, sinners and saints alike. Finally, in the supreme act of self giving love in death on a cross, God in Christ showed his presence in the world and affirmed the purpose and meaning of all life and history.

All Creation in Bondage to Sin and Death

The Confession of Faith says that "all persons rebel against God. . . and become slaves to sin and death" (2.04). It continues, "the alienation of persons from God affects the rest of creation, so that the whole creation stands in need of God's redemption" (2.06). Paul gave testimony concerning this bondage to sin and death: "Therefore, just as sin came into the world through one man, and death came through sin, and so death spread to all because all have sinned" (Rom. 5.12). Because of the sin of the human family, "the creation was subjected to futility," and is in "bondage to decay." (See Rom. 8:19-21.)

The story of the rebellion of the human family against God begins in the third chapter of Genesis. It is a story of brother murdering brother (Gen. 4:8), of a son deceiving his father (Gen. 27:5-29), of people enslaving people (Ex. 1:8-14), of a gang of men raping a defenseless woman (Ju. 19:22-26), of a king and his army devastating a country and killing all the men and boys, save one (1 Kings 11:14-17), of men and women violating their marriage vows and committing adultery (Hosea 4:14), and of governments oppressing their people (Isa. 3:13-15). One of the most poignant statements in all of Scripture appears when Genesis states that the earth was "corrupt in God's sight, and filled with violence," and that "the Lord was sorry that he made human kind on the earth, and it grieved him to his heart" (Gen. 6:6, 11).

The prophet Hosea describes the magnitude of the human family's rebellion against God and its effects on the rest of creation. Because of the absence of "knowledge of God in the land, . . . swearing, lying, stealing, and murder break out; bloodshed follows bloodshed. Therefore the land mourns, and all who live in it languish; together with the wild animals and the birds of the air, even the fish of the sea are perishing" (Ho. 4:2-3).

The stories of Scripture and their testimony to the impact of the sin of persons on the rest of creation bears a strong resemblance to stories on television's evening news, or on the front page of the daily newspaper. The story of violence, devastation, and destruction of the whole world, caused by the powers of sin and death, reaches its climax in the book of Revelation. (See Chapters 6-18.)Using the elaborate and complex imagery of apocalyptic literature, the writer gives a graphic description of the final but futile effort of the forces of evil to keep the whole creation in bondage to sin and death.

God's Judgment and Redemption

In the story of the Bible, an account of God's word in judgment and redemption overlays the account of the rebellion and sin of persons and the consequent bondage of the creation to sin and death. God does not abandon the creation, but continues an active presence in the events of nature and history. In a reference to the work of judgment and redemption through which God seeks to accomplish the divine will and purpose, not simply for the human family, but for all things, the Confession says, "God acts to heal the brokenness and alienation caused by sin" (3.01).

God will continue to uphold and nourish the creation until the divine purpose comes to consummation in God's time. Through judgment and redemption, God will ultimately set the creation free from bondage to sin and death. These two claims merge into one event in the second coming of Christ at the end of the age.

The Confession of Faith speaks of judgment and consummation, suggesting an integral relationship between the two events. The term judgment appears throughout Scripture, suggesting that it has been, since the appearance of the problem of sin, and continues to be an activity of God in human history. Scripture also speaks of a final judgment of God at the end of time. Thus the Confession says that "the judgment of God is both present and future" (7.05).

A fundamental question emerges immediately concerning the sense in which the Scripture uses the term judgment to describe God's dealings with sinful persons. If God's original covenant and continuing basic relationship with persons is legal in nature, then God's judgment is primarily a forensic or legal issue. In this sense, judgment becomes a divine act of law enforcement, bringing with it appropriate punishments for those guilty of breaking the law. In this sense judgment is punitive rather than redemptive. It brings death, not life.

On the other hand, if the original covenant and the continuing basic relationship between God and persons are based on grace, then God's judgment is a judgment of grace. The very title given to this commentary on the Confession of Faith, The *Covenant of Grace,* comes from the central claim of the Confession–that God's one and only covenant with the human family is a covenant of grace. (See COF 3.03.) In his teaching, his ministry to sinners, and his death on the cross, Jesus the Christ embodied the covenant of grace. This is the reason that John 3:16 stands at the very beginning of the text of the Confession.

God deals with persons as a parent in a family rather than as a judge in a court of law. Throughout human history, God's judgment has been for the purpose of redemption. It is an action in which God confronts persons with their sin, showing them its deadly consequences to themselves, to others, and to the whole creation. The Confession states that God abhors "war, civil strife, slavery, oppression, destruction of natural resources, political and economic exploitation . . . which cause needless suffering and death," (7.06) and confronts persons with their responsibility in such evils.

The judgment of grace does not impose a penalty of death, for the sinner has already received death as the wages of sin. Thus the Confession says that "persons experience God's judgment in . . . broken relationships with God and others, [and in] the guilt and consequences of their own actions" (7.05). The judgment of grace seeks to lead sinners to repentance, to faith and to life.

In human existence the ultimate judgment of God's grace was and continues to be manifested in the Cross. Here God in Christ confronts all persons with the awful consequences of their sins. Not only have they by their sins plunged themselves into bondage to death, they have also put to death the Savior of the world. The convicting power of the Cross increases with the realization that God in Christ suffered death willingly, as an act of self-giving, forgiving love. The awful truth of the Cross is that it is a judgment of love.

The final judgment at the end of time is a confirmation of God's judgment of grace in the events of nature and history. It emphasizes that the destinies of all persons in eternity are determined by their responses to God's judging and redeeming grace, which continually confronts them during their historical existence. The Confession states these truths very directly. Those persons who have responded to God's judgment of grace in repentance and faith "are assured of having passed from death of sin into life with God. They confidently await full redemption without fear of judgment" (7.04). On the other hand, "Those who reject God's salvation in Jesus Christ remain alienated from God in hopeless bondage to sin and death, which is hell" (7.07).

Jesus described the last judgment in the parable of the sheep and the goats in Matthew 25. However, the scene is not that of a courtroom, with people assembled to hear the judge pronounce their sentences. It is a scene beginning with a shepherd and a group of animals, and ending with a father determining who will and will not receive an inheritance as his children. What occurs is simply a separating out of the children of God (sheep), whom God told to enter into their inheritance of eternal life; from the children of the devil (goats), whom God told to enter into their inheritance of eternal death. The last judgment confirms both who they are, and that they have determined their destinies in eternity by their responses to the grace of God.

Death and Resurrection

The biblical understanding of the nature of persons is in contrast to the understanding found in ancient Greek philosophy and religion. These two views of the nature of persons differ radically and have important ramifications for understanding the sin and salvation of persons. It may be helpful in understanding the nature of the resurrection of the body to review the essential outlines of the Greek and biblical views of the nature of persons.

The Greek view is that a person is composed of two parts, a material body and an immaterial soul. The body and all its desires are essentially evil. The soul is essentially good. At birth a good soul becomes imprisoned in an evil body. At death the evil body simply dissolves into the matter from which it came, and the immaterial, immortal soul returns to heaven from which it came.

The biblical view is that a person is a unified self, not a dualism of body and soul. God created persons out of dust, and made them become living beings. (See Gen. 2:7.) An effort to understand the complex nature of persons necessitates references to body, mind, soul, spirit, will, and heart, but these terms simply serve as ways of talking about the complexity of the creature made in God's image. The apostle Paul sometimes talks about the flesh and the spirit, but he does not refer to the body and the soul in the Greek sense. Rather, he refers to the old, sinful person, and the new person in Christ.

A person sins, not a body. Sin destroys the unity of the self. Psychology describes this disunity as the self against the self. God redeems a person, not a soul. Redemption restores the unity of the self and is complete with the resurrection of the body from death. Scripture speaks of the creation of a new person, and of the resurrection of the person who is dead in sin.

During human life, the new person in Christ struggles with the remnants of the old person that had rebelled against God. Sanctification and growth in grace gradually purge these remnants of the old sinful self. The body, an integral part of the self, remains in the grip of death until the resurrection, which restores the complete unity of the person.

In an attempt to recognize both the complex nature and the essential unity of the person, the Confession says, "Death is both a spiritual and physical reality. . . . In Jesus Christ God acts to redeem persons from bondage to death both in spirit and body" (7.01). The redemption of persons is not complete until the resurrection of their bodies. Thus the Confession says, "Those who have been regenerated in Christ live with joyful and confident expectation that after death their redemption will be complete in the resurrection of the body" (7.02).

Scripture teaches that the redemption of persons is the creation of new persons–persons born of the Spirit. Extending the metaphor of being born again, the new person in Christ becomes a child in the family of God. Such a person has already in some sense entered into eternity. The person has received the gift of eternal life. In some sense, the person is already in heaven with God, for the nature of the Christian life is that it allows people to live with God, daily walking and talking with God.

In this life, constant fellowship in the family of God suffers from the limitations of the remains of the old self, and from the sinful conditions of the world. Death removes these limitations and believers enter into a new level of fellowship with God, a new dimension of heaven. The resurrection of the body removes the last remnant of bondage to sin and death. As children of God, persons achieve wholeness and maturity, living joyfully with God in the family of God throughout eternity.

A parallel understanding of persons who are and remain in bondage to sin and death exists. These persons are not only in danger of dying and going to hell, in some sense they are in hell already. They live in bondage to the powers of evil and cannot set themselves free. The Confession of Faith describes the magnitude of this bondage when it states that such persons are "inclined toward sin in all aspects of their being" (2.03).

Through the Holy Spirit, God calls all persons out of bondage to sin and death and into freedom and life with God. God confronts persons with their sin and rebellion, and seeks by the judgment of love to create in them the responses of repentance and faith. Those who continue throughout their lives on earth to reject the call of the Holy Spirit and who persist in their rebellion against God will die in bondage to sin and death. At the end of time this bondage will be made complete, when they are resurrected to eternal death, "which is hell." (See Jn. 5:28-29; COF 7.07.)

The Consummation of the Kingdom of God

The Scripture uses the metaphors of kingship, rule, and kingdom to describe God's activity in the events of nature and history. In one sense the entire creation constitutes a realm over which God rules. In a more particular sense, the covenant community is a people over whom God rules. The rule of God is another way of talking about how God goes about accomplishing the divine will and purpose in all of creation and in the covenant community.

To say that God consummates all life and history means that at the end of time God's purpose will prevail on earth as it prevails in heaven. The Confession looks forward to the consummation of history, and says that "at the coming of Jesus Christ the kingdoms of this world shall become the kingdom of the Lord and of the Christ, and he shall reign forever and ever" (7.08).

The prophets of the Old Testament developed the concept of the Kingdom of God, and interpreted the nature of God's rule. They saw clearly that the will of God was not being done on earth as it is always being done in heaven. They called the covenant community to repentance and to a more perfect obedience of the will of God. The prophets were the first to talk about a person whom God would anoint to establish the perfect rule of God and to usher in a new age.

In response to the message of the prophets, the people of the covenant community began to look expectantly for the coming of the Realm of God, the beginning of the messianic age. Tragically, they mistook the metaphors of king and kingdom for literal descriptions of the Messiah and converted the messianic promise into a nationalistic hope. When the Messiah finally came and began to rule, most of the people of the covenant community, especially its leaders, considered him an imposter.

Today, the covenant community looks expectantly for the second coming of the Messiah and the consummation of his kingdom. Tragically, many in the covenant community still mistake the metaphorical language of such books as Revelation for literal description of the consummation of the Kingdom of God and create false expectations concerning this event. Nevertheless, the Scripture is clear when it says that with the second coming of the Messiah there will be a new creation, a new heaven and a new earth. (See Rev. 21:1.) The new creation will not exist in time and space, but in eternity. Revelation describes it as the New Jerusalem, in which the "temple is the Lord God almighty and the Lamb" (Rev. 21:1, 22).

Changing metaphors, Revelation describes this event as a marriage between Christ and the church. (See Rev. 19:1-10; 21:1-2). A family celebration follows: "See, the home of God is among mortals. He will dwell with them as their God; they will be his people, and God himself will be with them; and he will wipe every tear from their eyes" (Rev. 21:3-4). Alluding to the original creation, the Scripture says that the new creation will have a "tree of life; . . . and the leaves of the tree will be for the healing of the nations" (Rev. 22:2). There will be no need for lamp or sun, "for the Lord God will be their light, and they shall reign forever and ever" (Rev. 22:5).

For Discussion

1. Why does Scripture say that God created the world and all that is in it?
2. What claim does Scripture make concerning the impact of the sin of persons on the world and all that is in it?
3. What is the nature of God's judgment and redemption, through which Scripture says God will accomplish the divine purpose in creation?
4. What do you understand the Scripture to teach about the doctrine of the resurrection of the body?
5. How do you react to the claim that the end of the age, like the resurrection of Jesus, will occur on the border line between time and eternity? What is the purpose of such a claim?
6. How do you feel about the questions the Confession leaves unanswered concerning the consummation of history? How do you respond to people in other traditions who insist on more concrete answers to questions concerning the end of life as we know it?

About the Author

HUBERT WILLIAM MORROW

Hubert W. Morrow (1922-2007) was an ordained minister in the Cumberland Presbyterian Church. He held degrees from Bethel College (now University) and Vanderbilt University. He was a member of Arkansas Presbytery.

He and his wife, Virginia Sue Williamson Morrow, had two children: Mary Sue, a college music professor, and David, on ordained minister. There are three grandchildren. Nathan, Joel, and Andrew Morrow.

Dr. Morrow served a number of pastorates. He was employed as executive secretory of the Board of Missions and Evangelism from 1950 to 1954. He was elected Moderator of the General Assembly of the Cumberland Presbyterian Church in 1956. From 1957-1974. he was on the faculty of Bethel College as Professor of Religion and Philosophy. Dr. Morrow become associate professor of Missions and Historical Theology and director of Continuing Education at Memphis Theological Seminary In 1980. He served as Academic Dean of Memphis Theological Seminary from 1981 until 1988. After retirement he continued to serve the church as a writer, speaker, and teacher in the Program of Alternate Studies.

In 1977 the General Assembly of the Cumberland Presbyterian Church voted to initiate a revision of the *Confession of Faith* of 1883. Dr. Hubert Morrow served as a member of the committee of 21 persons to implement the work of revision.

Made in the USA
Lexington, KY
14 September 2015